RHYMES of a PFC

RHYMES of a PFC

BY **Lincoln Kirstein,** ASN 32807032

NEW DIRECTIONS, *New York*   JOHN WEATHERHILL, INC., *Tokyo*

AUTHOR'S NOTE

This book of fragments is neither documentation nor autobiography. With the exception of well-known public figures, whose deeds are now matters of history, all characters (and not least those speaking in the first person) are contrived composites, drawn more from imagination than from actual experience. Any similarity in the use of names or physical attributes to people living or dead is accidental.

Published in the United States by NEW DIRECTIONS, *Norfolk, Connecticut, and 333 Sixth Avenue, New York City 14; and in Japan by* JOHN WEATHERHILL, INC., *50 Ryudo-cho, Azabu, Minato-ku, Tokyo | Copyright © 1964 by Lincoln Kirstein; all rights reserved | Printed in Japan | Library of Congress Catalog Card No. 64–21142 | First edition, October, 1964.*

TABLE OF CONTENTS

France

Germany

Postscript

Prologue

FALL IN

My mother's brother hauled me to the big-boys' club,
 Where they swam nude, drank beer, shared secrecy.
Males young and old held mystic privilege.
 I was condemned to join their mystery.

These men were hairy on belly and groin;
 The boys were hairier at least than me,
No boy, no man, a neuter in-between,
 One hairless silly, neither he nor she.

In locker room my uncle stripped me raw.
 My shyness shivered at his shameless, bare,
Terrible body. Off he tore my drawers
 And shoved me naked to the brink of where

In a tiled cage they'd sunk their sacred pool,
 Clean as a toilet bowl, its water poison-green;
No mama near to save or cry "Forbear!"
 The taste of infamy is sweet chlorine.

I knew that death swam near but hated uncle more.
 If I were doomed, then uncle, he must pay.
I'd scream, I'd make a scene, or the extreme:
 I'd plummet to bottom, midget martyr play

Profoundly drowned, which simply took despair
 (Distinct from courage since it involved caprice),
Hold my breath to bursting waiting The End.
 In suicide is blackmail and release.

3

He tugged me out with terror, even awe.
   I felt my fright infect his grizzled chest;
Palpating this drowned rat to retch and drain,
   He knew I knew who'd flunked his foolish test.

Thus one bears fear in action, guilt in pride.
   I was his sister's son, yet still no male.
The spineless kin he'd vowed to make a man
   Confounded polity and saw him fail.

The rage of armies is the shame of boys;
   A hero's panic or a coward's whim
Is triggered by nerve or nervousness.
   We wish to sink. We do not choose to swim.

WORLD WAR I

Du *bist der Kaiser Wilhelm!* Thy Huns shall rue our blame.
Dad teaches us to hate thee. It is a stirring game.
   On the back of a Cuban cigar box the scowl of Kaiser Bill
   Embossed upon its glossy lid evokes a ritual thrill.

On many a night, just before bed, we gravely open it.
Upon thy iron moustachios Dad, I, and my brother spit.
   Dad's parents both were German; so were Mama's too;
   His pair poor, her pair rich, pure types of German Jew.

Dad's folks came here from Prussia in 1848
With Karl Schurz and some exiles, and not one day too late.
    Dad sent me my first postcard—*Der Brandenburgertor*—
    With guardsmen in spiked helmets—*Kronprinzens Elite Korps*—

Whose officers when off parade mock tourists touring town,
And when they smell like German Jews, they knock my daddy down.
    Hence now we needs must trounce them with witchcraft and with gun
    Who skewer Belgian babies and rape old nuns for fun,

Which I learn from thrilling pamphlets cooked up by staunch George Creel,
Though it's sex more than compassion that I truly really feel.
    German spies spy *everywhere*. Ma swears our neighbor's Fräulein
    Signals from a Marblehead Beach her secret submarine-sign.

Karl Muck conducts the symphony; a steel svelte villain, he—
Ma says he's Wagner's bastard son ("Daddy, what's *bastardy?*")—
    Conducts "The Star Spangled Banner" in clearly treasonous style.
    Mother shrewdly decodes this, watching his back the while.

Our weather's *mighty peculiar*: clouds rarely rain; they *pour*.
Phenomenon caused by bombardment, in this our first World War.
    We save sticky peach pits, too, 'mongst other momentous tasks,
    Which by chemistry or alchemy are rendered for gas masks.

Our scout master, Harvard '17, enlists at the very first
Of Pershing's call for volunteers. Ah, that day is the worst
    When he takes leave of us, his lads, who pray he may not die;
    We partake of sarsaparilla and a splendid communal cry.

Joe, my father's office boy, whose acne spoils an angel face,
Turns up for Sunday supper in the guest of honor's place
    Scrubbed beet-red, immaculate, in manlike sailor-white.
    I'm ten years old. I love him dear. His uniform is Navy tight.

My pa is past an age to fight, but everyone else we know
Plays his irreplaceable part against an implacable foe
    Save Earl O'Toole, the janitor, mulatto with much progeny,
    My first preceptor in the lore of absolute necessity.

Earl shows me things and tells me things I'm not supposed to know,
But without my knowing or being shown, how'm I expected to grow?
    Curiosity kills no nine-lived cats. It's true. Can I ever repay
    Him for his grand advisements? He discovers a practical way.

In wars the rich are warm enough, the poor frequently cold.
Anthracite or bituminous fuel may not be bought or sold,
    Yet with a magic ticket got from he won't say where
    They hand me chunky bags of coal simply for standing there,

In a queue of wives in shawls with kids, gath'ring before the light,
Shuffling through steel-shovel forenoon deep into slip-ice night.
    I'm well aware of my tailor-made togs: reefer of Harris tweed
    Betrays an interloper's lack of legal material need.

But I'm Earl's apt apprentice and shall double for his dole,
And I'm O'Toole's accomplice who'll cotch him rationed coal.

An end to battles boiling peach pit, mustard gas, and blood.
Kaiser and Clown Prince in exile take turns at sawing wood.

Scout Master's back at college. I'm sent away to school.
Pondering all my prayers for him, I sorta feel a fool.

This World War turns out to be only the first World War,
A problem for teachers to tackle without making it seem a bore,
But gleaming through forty-five winters I see by a coal-gas fire
A tutor telling me better than my own shy tongue-tied sire:

His marbled mulatto eyeballs, half Irish, half African:
Earl, he demonstrates on me how is it you make a man.

W ABC

War leaves some half-shot young men
Who wage it, get wounded, and then
Take long aimless walks through the night.

I learned this, if I recall right,
Somewhere between twelve and thirteen,
When, precociously keen,
My family all safely asleep,
I dreamed up appointments to keep,
Got up and got dressed in the dark
To walk down that broad strip of park
On Commonwealth Avenue,
Block after block through light dew.

Elms fanned above the wide mall
Giving scale to their big and my small;
Street names spelled an odd alphabet
Whose rubric I'll never forget:

Arlington, Berkeley, Clarendon,
Dartmouth, Exeter, Fairfield, on
Past Gloucester to Hereford, where
I picked up a well-deserved scare.

A trench-coated man tapped a cane—
Canadian ex-soldier in pain
Inhaled the dank airs of the night.
Like me, he couldn't sleep tight.

My prowls in a tom-kitten youth
Pursued some vague personal truth,
Though often my daddy warned me
Against living dangerously:
I was not to risk the fierce morn
Nor discover how or why I was born.

Yet here I was early, and met
A sleep-walking loony. You bet
He was bats: a classical case
Since he lacked a third of his face.
His folks owned that château and tree
This side Fairfield at Newbury.

I shadowed him mutely around,
Out of sight but not out of sound,

Though he was too far gone to care
For some curious kid staring there—
Shy me playing sly Sherlock Holmes,
Protecting the health of our homes
From a typical type of shell shock.

If only two fellows could talk.

But he was oblivious of me
Envious of maturity;
Me drawn, hot, aching and wild,
Half a man, to him, half a child—
Me plotting great war books on where
"Over the Top" 's "Over There,"
Though I'd been nowhere but here,
Damp in teen-age erotics of fear.

I stole strength from his adult shell shock
Past each alphabetical block.
A-B-C spells L-O-V-E:
Mayn't I magic his blindness to see?
I wasn't his dad nor his son;
My own epic had barely begun.
Hence I was content me to stalk
My wounded stag rock over rock:

Exeter, Dartmouth, Clarendon,
By Berkeley to Arlington,
While he led the perilous way
Past Arras, Bapaume, and Cambrai.

Stateside

BASIC TRAINING

Belvoir! What's war to someone who's never known war before?
> Our Civil War—
Splendid in springtime, a sprightly gift sent us from worlds away;
> Under rubbery clay,
Popping out of Virginia hills, coral-pink bushes bud; thrushes sing,
Stirring our fuzzy green fresh clean wildly promising
> Tender marvelous May.

Eighty years gone, more or less, all these roads ran to Bull Run,
> But now our fun
Apes a miniature shadow of such vast disaster to spot
> A few snapshots of what
We've come to suspect has little to do with wars we ever shall see
Fought on land or sea: tanks; planes. No horse cavalry,
> Minié ball, nor grapeshot.

Yet my civil war's nearer than that war over the blue:
> World War II,
Which means zero to me save for drab facts which inspire me to fear;
> I'm absurdly quite here
Trying hard to pretend our crack halfback lieutenant, Bill Beady Eye,
Risks a charge under raking cross fire to let fly
> Carbines and a thin cheer.

This weak dull pun on battles our schoolbook creates
> Between the States;
Where First Massachusetts and Third Tennessee pitched scarecrow tents,
> They've hewn stone monuments.

Better than Brady in albums, a leap towards historical fact
Is fooling with live ammunition, trying to re-enact
            Real warlike sentiments.

What sort of an officer's Bill Beady Eye? He's all right—
            By a damn sight
No West Point paladin, Stonewall, Stuart, or Lee. Full of zest,
            Does his beady-eyed best
To haul our poor amateur ranks up a knoll he insists we must take.
Victory! It's took. He awards us a ten-minute break.
            I relax with the rest

And try to recall Dick Hales, a boy I'd known since a child:
            Meek was, and mild.
His dad, a drunk, tossed him his cavalry saber; quit home for worse.
            Dick, a sissy of course,
Tacked the sword to his wall, whimpered for Mummy to come and be kissed;
Never won games nor a girl; to Canada crossed to enlist
            In their Royal Air Force.

Yesterday, in some clippings from home I chanced to have read
            Dick Hales is dead.
Slid his flakked plane sidewise low over Sussex to spare a girls' school;
            No trick for coward or fool.
He had the presence of heart or head to make his enormous bet.
Now is he hero, haloed and holy. His mummy can get
            Used to life's being cruel.

Dick: what is left of you now, with my civil war please coincide.
            Kidding aside,

Accept sprig of apple or plum which pitiless April has brought,
　　　The meager tribute I've got;
First to fall among men I have known, always sure to get hit—
Or, after the fact, seems so—your crash links history a bit:
　　　Minié ball, flak, grapeshot.

BARRACKS

I couldn't swing a pass tonight and hitch to town; it doesn't mean
　　I'm punished. Desk-sergeant fills his wretched quota early.
　　Restricted to the post—frustrated, nervous, surly,
I'll cruise the enlisted-men's canteen.

Nothing doing. One ping-pong table busted; last week's *Time* and *Life;*
　　Debris depicting a tattered still-life of sullen fun
　　To fill a futile evening; time-off barely begun,
Back to barracks; write the little wife.

Steam overheats our barn. In the latrine's firm Lysol smell and taste,
　　Radio blaring, one dumb Polack buffs his brilliant shoes
　　Already shined; rub and snap mark time to grimy blues.
No choice endows us but puny waste.

Safe and sound *in vacuo*, this side of oceans which run to blood,
　　We've no right to brood on boredom as disaster.
　　Genuine adversity hurls its iron verdict faster;
We dabble idly in the rising flood

Of imminent change. Stiff in double layers down our hollow hall,
   Blank beds accuse each tardy, lost, or absent candidate
   Off whoring. Boxed in bed, the tossing wakers wait
Late tumblings-in, curse, or beer-born call—

Revenge on early sleepers. Wide eyed, resist all simple slumber.
   Self-pity's smothered tantrum disguised as dogged sorrow
   Postpones reveille until abrupt tomorrow
Indicts us for Name, Serial Number,

And Shipment Overseas. Bongo thunder, penny-scattered rain
   Caress mute victims whose feeble protest faints to snore or groan.
   Wifeless but warm in woolen, hugging skin and bone,
Nurse counterfeit despair as sterling pain.

MAP & COMPASS

We city kids have quit the town
   In search of Mrs. Nature.
   We seek her nomenclature,
Abandoned since our Boy Scout youth
Which still proclaims poetic truth:
   How starry winkers prickle night
   Till frail pink dawn slams strong sunlight
On ground that's not macadam black but rock-rib green or brown.

The stay-at-homes fill featherbed;
  They lie there softly dozing,
  While here I am exposing
Extremity of toe and nose
To smashing sunup's crimson rose,
  A spectacle unseen for years;
  And as for song, my rousèd ears
Hear counter-tenor cockerel to raise me from the dead.

Bivouac's an ancient cossack hut
  Remaindered from a war
  That took its toll before
We knew a thing. Now they teach us
New techniques for the present fuss,
  Indoctrinating tenderfeet
  For hide-and-seek advance, retreat,
By drilling civil eye and ear to fortify the gut.

Here is my compass; here's a map
  With cryptic markings on it.
  For mystic marathon, it
Posits by curving contour plan
The progress for a partisan.
  We're not draftees, man. We are men,
  Range riders chasing the Cheyenne,
Or cop and robber, hot at heel of Jerry or of Jap.

I cannot spot magentic north;
  My needle dances madly.
  I draw a sketch map badly.

To ask for help is worse than sin;
We're on our own from here on in—
      Coördinates a keyless code;
      I'll *never* hit that sunken road.
A bird-brain nitwit, spoiled at school, my fame shall be henceforth.

I call it quits to take a walk
      In mild June's wildwood weather.
      A rooster's of my feather,
Brass cackling in the forest park.
His master is a hermit dark
      Whose shack is stacked in tamarack.
      He bids me in to share a snack,
Corn pone, pot likker, turnip greens, and smooth didactic talk.

Here I admit to being lost.
      We agree, for he's lost too,
      Or hidden from common view
Of men at war; loves beast and bird,
Enjoys their noise, credits their word,
      No newspaper, nor radio;
      A neighbor store's where he can go
To get him food, drug, tobacco at no tremendous cost.

I put my compass in his hand.
      It makes precious little sense;
      Equally, we two are dense.
I spread my map upon his floor;
As far as sense goes, this makes more.

He knows his terrain like no one
And shows me what I should have done
By longitude or latitude. Armed with such contraband

I hit my sunken road, right smack
On the button, way ahead
Of wise guys who've only read
Compass and map as their textbook.
Hence I'll take me a longer look
At Mrs. Nature's gazetteer,
Hoping that through the wars I'll steer
No path a map or compass trick to take me off my track.

CADETS

August and you two sting our salty eyes:
A brisk couple, seasonably dressed,
Lean, virginal. Such pairing mystifies
Even sophisticates; we are impressed.
But what to call you? Must you be addressed
As officers? Cucumber-cool bearing
Kindles a nimbus churlishly caressed
By our limp envy, nor are you caring
For any flat, basebred, furtive staring.

We are draftees, by lottery chosen;
      Protesting vaguely, we surrendered hands,
Heads, and hearts, reserving souls as frozen
      Against all terminal extreme commands.
      You volunteered. Despotic whole demands
Upon your sacred persons or honors
      Enhance a ducal air which here withstands
All error, disciplining you owners
Of feudal grace—its stewards and donors.

Under leathern vizard, immaculate shirt,
      Strict pants, bright boots, taut belt, firm pumiced chin—
Abstainers from vernaculars of dirt,
      Dapper braced greyhounds—your careers begin
      On us, a mongrel kind, since our coarse skin
Proclaims another breed, closer to earth.
      In our twin truce we've but one war to win,
Delaying measurement of common worth
And confident we share no common birth.

West Point made you; your granite mother,
      Cliff nestled and rock mantled, tinged your sight
Its armored glint. Each grey cloistered brother
      Disdains endearment, taking his delight
      In stern alliance for the handy fight;
Friends we may never be. Our slack buddies
      Console us all en masse. Cadets incite
Us to tricks past individual studies—
War's homework, boring before it bloodies.

2

Second Lieutenants, your crisp commissions
    A fortnight granted, to Belvoir take you,
Subaltern instructors, where traditions
    Frame the tribal rites wherein we'll rake you
    With ready wit and rude, yet it shan't shake you,
Expert at hazing and inured to this.
    Foolish conceit to bet we'd ever break you:
Our duel initiates with an armistice—
Courage at odds with inverse cowardice

To prove us both professional. As when
    We play the game to build a Bailey Bridge:
No officers; noncoms, enlisted men,
    Choosing an ill-considered anchorage
    For both abutments. On a backdrop ridge
Stylish West Pointers overlook the scene,
    Amused, no doubt; vaunting their privilege
By nice withdrawal. Sidewise, watch them lean
Fancy, against a fence, as if to preen

Their eaglet plumage. Sodden in midstream
    The home team wrangles crisscross-bolted steel—
Two dozen raw ambitious paws. Blaspheme
    The martial law under whose mucky heel
    We flop hip-high in mud, and no appeal
To extra aid. A section slips an inch,
    One inch is all. Frail caryatids feel
Dead hefty tonnage slide, and it's a cinch
Our pipestem backbones won't support the pinch

Of backbreak lock. Buckling, we stoop to founder.
      Sharp yells and thrashing wavelets snap their lash
On drifters whose twelve spent shoulders flounder.
      Tendons splinter to a supple mishmash
      Of muscle. Our span, staggering to its splash,
Lurches. Disaster depends on metal.
      Two dive, with swift reliable panache:
Cadets hop in to calibrate their mettle,
Grasping that wrought-iron flower, the nettle,

Safety. So what? We'd have won without you
      And shall insist you were never needed
Though some quicksilver sleight-of-hand about you—
      Even had you never interceded
      On our behalf—claims you both stampeded
Towards realms above the silly stink of swank;
      Neccessity herself you fair exceeded
In pure exuberance of valor's prank,
Though such fine manners we are slow to thank.

Later, with whisky-sodas at your club
      We bet you bask in congratulations—
Baptism by fire—and were we there we'd snub
      Your champion clique's cavalier citations—
      We, envious of luxury rations:
Good alcohol and praise. In warm showers
      We'll cherish bruise and welt. Niggard nations
Compete by pattern; pelts tell our story.
You saved our skins. We grudge you this glory.

GLORIA

If you doan mind, would you please Mind moving over, *please*.
Thank YOU. There's Plenty of room for All us girls. Jeez,
    hon, I'm Sorry; really. So how should *I* know. I thought
    we was All girls here, though now I see you are Not
but can take the Joke. What a Relief! For about One
second I was scared you'd Sock me; but honest, hon,
    you Do remind me of Someone I knew years ago:
    just your type although you yourself might'n think so—

I mean super-fishulee—crew cut, all your
Classs. It's that clean-cut Navy Look; it always sure
    beats Me, though I was Army, but it wasn't the Real me.
    I adore Navy. The Most. The U.S. Navy—
but what admiral would want me? I'm asking you, man:
does this Interest you? Oh, you, Stop! So…I can
    pro-ceed? Sometimes it's quite Hard to know who is honestly
    inerstid. Fred was the First I knew when he

Joins the Navy and such a Good Kid, naughty but nice,
wild And cute; wicked, he's just the kind you look Twice
    at, but he never got into no trouble Untillll
    he was in Service. Then, mann, did he get his Fillll!
This all Begins *Years* before, but let's Skip all that;
I was living in a little cold-water flat;
    I was being Alone, then. Fred, sometimes, spent the night;
    he was working Out of Town and doing All Right—

Sold National Advertising for some Large Concern,
not High Pay but he was just beginning to Learn.
    One day, we weren't even At War yet, he wanders in;
    "Gloria," he grins, "I dood it." He done it, En-
listed. I was Dumb-Founded. I gave him a big kiss;
We got Screamin. Imagine! In *Uniform* This
    One would look like sheer Mad heaven; simply cannot beat
    your Navy blue-and-gold or that old Navy neat-

Nessss. You All look ssoo Damn *clean*. Why does Army *never*
in spite of all them soapy showers look Ever
    clean? Fred done his first bootcamp bit way out at Great Lakes.
    Tough, but made it— WAIT! Your're Leaving! Now, for Land sakes,
You need One More Beer. Now *please*. This one's on Meee. Now then. . .
I lost my apartment. Bitchy landlady, when
    I spend Weeks ripping plaster, Complete two-coat painting,
    and Entire interior Ree-Decorating—

The Back Room apple-green, trim in Black; the front, a brick wall
hung with a *Huge* baroque mirror. Sooo, after all
    this, she raise the Rent. She said I wasn't a good Bet.
    I paid on the Dot. I should be living there Yet.
But let's not talk about Meee. Fred's at Norfolk, now onnn.
I didn't hear One word for Weeks. I thought; he's GONE
    and Shipped Out, but then, smack: in the middle of the Night
    a *telegram* phones. It's from Fred all right, all right.

"Come Norfolk At Once. *Difficulties*." My Poor dear Fred.
I couldn't sleep a Wink, just lay Thinking, in bed   **24**

And scared Green, and I mean for Himmm, not at all for Meee....
By mistake he'd written a Letter, you seee....
To my Old addresss, since he hadn't my New addressss—
Wrote on the envelope his *Own* address. I guesss
    That landlady Did it, but we'd never rightfully Know;
    it was opened by Errorr. I never saw it, though

Fred said it was Something Like as how he'd Met this Marrr-
velous mahogany-haired marine, some Gay Barrr,
    and went up In Smoke. It *worked*. And this young kid Liked Fred;
    sensational. Fred went out of his fucking Headdd,
drew his profile for me: crew cut, big jaw, cute lad;
Fred was a good draftsman; the Firm he worked for had
    thought him Talented for layouts. He sketched Very Good;
    he could have been a Great Illustrator, he could.

His letter must have been One Wow of a camperooo
with this marine's Portrait and Full Description tooo
    describing Everything. What's this letter do Then?
    Gets itself turned over to CID—you know: Those Men
who confront Fred with it, without Warning, just like That:
"*You* Wrote This?" His own commanding officer asked: "What
    is the Meaning of *this?*" Fred said: "Well, sir, it don't Meannn
    Nothing. It's just a Joke—in Bad Taste." Get that quean.

Who'd believe Fred? There wasn't One small Shadow of doubt
what his Whole silly sincere letter was About.
    They didn't exactly Arrest him; held him Confined
    in the best hotel. He started to Lose his Mind,

wired Meee. Then, it wasn't easy to catch a plane quick:
Norfolk, wartime, two-motor plane. I was Quite sick:
    I get sick when it's at all bumpy, sometimes when Not.
    I thought: Gloria, if Ize in some Christless spot

Who'd I turn to? Fred, natch. So the Least poor I could do—
try and help Himmm. Hotel room in Norfolk with *Whooo*
    but a marine guard. Get the Picture? I had to get
    permission from his commandant before they'd let
me Innn. They left the door Open so they could listen and
needn't Buggg it. Now I begin to Understand
    it's a Court-Martial offenssse; but—they better Be Sure
    and Prove it. Just get us a good lawyer, but your

Sainted Mother now found that Some people are just Viiile.
They had No idea of letting Fred stand trialll;
    without no Prrooof, just this letter and sketch, like Fred said:
    a joke; in rather poor Taste. Fred was real well bred;
slips me a note: tells me: "Go this certain gay bar Where"
his marine would sure probably Beee—but when?—there-
    sooo, if Anyone asked Questions not to say One Thing,
    quel horreur, though Fred said Jack would Nnneverrr sing.

I'll do anything for Friends, but I didn't know:
What Could I do? CID watched wherever I'd go;
    Was this *smart?* I'm a sensible girl; curious, too,
    how this one would Look, for Fred's a Real Expert and you
Are curious when somebody's Gorgeous. You wanta Seee.
I'm only Human: would this, his, Jack—be for Meee?

Hon... Bar was filled with mad numbers. Remember the Warrr?
Like a friggin floor show. But no Jack. I drank farrr

Into the night. Next morning I saw Fred, my poor friend,
in a Horrible state. He looked just like the *End*.
    Those lousy CID's. What had they now Gone and Done?
    You wouldn't Believe it. My grey hair *curled*. That SON
of a bitch the marine guard who brung in poor Fred's food
wasn't allowed to talk to him; this same guy who'd
    been sent in last night, late, with an old hospital tray:
    milk and fruit; then this marine slips Away.

At the time Fred didn't notice. He was too Down to eat—
finds on his plate a thoughtful extra-added Treattt:
    a loaded service revolver. Man, I never knew
    what the old United States Navy could *do* to you.
Soooo ... your Sainted Mother had Quite a time keeping Fred
From putting a bullet through his pretty head.
    I pleaded with him, begged really: the best I could;
    they'd nothing on him At All; so What is the good

In *Suicide?* He wrote a letter. Assuming it's true
(which it was)—it's not the First time. It's nothing New.
    But Fred Collapsed. He broke down. He cried, he cried and cried.
    But no hari-kari. I saw his captain, Lied
like a real character witness, though I couldn't quite telll
what Cap thought. Told him about Fred's broads. Oh welll....
    I got down on my Kneeess. I prayed for Common Sense.
    This captain, splendid man, loved Fred; was just Immense;

Said Fred was a good man for a good job—in his Way;
told me, very kind: Go back. You tell him: O.K.
    they'd fix something up, but for High Heaven's Sweet Sake
    don't write no more *Letters*. This time he'd get a break.
This puts hope into Freddy-boy. He cheers up a bit,
saw the light; then on in we laughed a lot at it.
    I smuggled beer; gave some to that marine guard and he
    winked. From then on in, it went rather Easily.

But Fred had an Idea proving he's not so Bright;
in some ways he's stupid. Now he thought it all right
    since he's in the Clear and since I had to get Back
    (I was just a working girl, didn't want the sack),
I should cruise that bar again, try to make One last try,
see if I could actually contact this guy;
    couldn't Bear to think he'd never see Junior anywhere.
    How'd I tell which jack Jack was with all them jacks there?

But he needn't ask mother *twice*. I went. Found myself one
Sensational number. No kin to Jack, though *fun*.
    We had beers. You can't help try to make some Try.
    I didn't tell Fred. Him so Depressed. Why should I?
That's about *It*. Today, he'll still say I saved his life;
us camping, I cast myself as his divorced wife,
    we kid about Him paying Me my own alimony....
    End of Story? Not quite. (One more beer?)... I agree:

Hasn't much *Point*. That's The point of this here story:
they let him resign for the good of Old Glory.

Soooo ... then what does this Foooll do? Joins the Marines, he does:
    Ferocious combat training. It was
Murder. Shave you. Beat you. Feed you live ammunition.
Fred did great. He had military ambition.
    So then some Bastard dug up his old Papers and found
    his Navy Records and, natch, they could make it sound

Bad. Marines chuck him out. You think That's it? You ain't seen
Nothing yet. Sooo, now he joins the merchant marine:
    him a mere merchant seaman after all he's been Through.
    Then They got his records Too. They chuck him out Toooo.
My poor Freddy was now a three-time loser for Keeps.
He gave up. I got drafted but you needn't weep
    for your Sainted Mother. Europe? A Ball, for three years.
    Fred? Took it like a Man. Shed no more tears,

Just sat the rest of This war out. Grim fairy tale?
Fred a failure? No, sir, though I watched him fail
    three times, perfectly cast as that Navy juvenile,
    adoring the Service, a good officer, while
when I spoke to his sweet commandant I *did* get Notions
that old salt Liked Fred. Honest, hon, the fucking ocean's
    Fulll of Strange fish. After the war, Fred makes more than me,
    a first-rate illustrator and No tragedy.

I see him less when I get back from Over Seas. . . .
Now—you Leaving? Please, hon; please. Sir, one more. Sir. Please.

SYKO

Doc Young says I got new roses   hell   new roses he says
You ought to hear the questions he ask me   doc   I said
You the one thats nuts not me   he said

Sex shun 8   what did I do crazy Id like to know
I socked Hansen   what was I suppose to do   if you
was me I bet you sock Hansen too

I try to be nice   lookit   I dont want no fight never
He pick on me from the first   he didn like my face
Well   I didn like his ugly face

One night we get frenl and intmat   talking   I mean
I told him things I nevr told no one before
It was a load off my mind   whats more

He told me stuff I never heard talked out loud at all
I guess it was true and so if you think the word friend
means anything we were friends

One day skuttlebut   all them roomers said we had to move
Half of us moving so the other half have to stay
I start to worry   half night all day

Would Hansen stay or would Hansen ship out   would he leave me
No one knew   Hansen didn know   did he wanta go
or stay   I hoped he woodn go

Then he start act so mean he woodn even say hi
    Some times I followd him round askn what I done
    Done   he said   done   just leave me all own

Thats it   leave him all own   so I leave him so   I doan care
    if thats the way he wants it   who does he think he is
    Just a big dumb swede   thats who he is

It turns out to be true   they decide to ship Hansen out
    I see his name posted and my name not on the list
    But mite have been   howd I get missed

I hunt for Hansen for I want to know if he new
    He had his bag and gear laid out on his bunk almost packed
    I stood there   I said   no   thing   he cracked

some wise crack how glad he was to get ship out   he said more
    a lot more   too much   I took it but then saw red
    If I hit him harder   hed   be   d

So I didn hit him too hard because he hit me right back
    We trade punch and he could hit real good   I let him hit
    me   it felt good   like the man said   it

feels good after you stop hitting a brick wall with your head
    I fell on his sack   after he gone I will take on his bed
    Partings sweet sorrow   like the man said

One collossal punch and GOD   witness fratercideal site
    He woodn let His boy down   HE show of in bright light
    a commando knife right there   we fight

Batteries flushing evil from my overtack brain
    short circuit so I got to getem recharge again
    My blood circulate back ward in vain

I zoom to top level level   find all tough problems clear
    Trees are more green   birds galore   DOGS o so near an DEER
    An no snak cree ping in con flick or f e a r

All con flicx are with my s e l f and atually may I so o o n die
    My big trubl alway sbin with I I I   I   I
    I never find no wors averseraye

Whil GOD love me me me Me Me ME ME Me he says Hansens my angl brothr
    and I must pass if eye him from evry othr
    for we was born from the sam Mother MOTHER M O T   H

GOD   GOD   GOD say so an god GOD has ME rkuperatin in thjs plajc
    But he stars to luck lik ths doc ter hjs fajc
    r semb ls doc YOUNG while thjs ratracje

they run half lik a hrspitl hav like FRESNO jail
    A gang o skinjy nurses wid no tit and no tale
    GOD   GOD forget me   I rcjeev no mail

I dree dreeaem Th SACRET   HEARTJEEZZ in rubbeez o flam fire
    But not in blackan white in tekncolr SHE   I desr
    What you think I am some lousy liar?????

Just kayn rember how they got ME put awa
    NXQRRT $ % # say I am coprting lts betr ech da
    & whr in hel is HANSEN any waaaaa # &&&

OBSTACLE COURSE

Here we are now, all well or ill met,
Quite sure this isn't It—not yet.
We wait, steady on. Get set
    For the obstacle course.

It is sampling of battle in small,
Lacking crisis or casual,
Practical dress rehearsal
    Of invasion in force.

Master sergeant and brass hang around
Overlooking tank trap and mound,
Swamp, quicksand—treacherous ground
    To try untried recruits

Handicapped in this steeple chase.
Desk, shop, farm was hardly the place
To train for so fleet a pace
    Shod in thick combat boots;

Too spavined or puny for such game,
But age, weight, height, color, or name
Each screens his riddle the same:
    Will I make it or not?

On your mark. Ready. Get set. Now: go!
Pistols crack; police whistles blow.
Careless run fast, cautious slow,
    Ambling off at a trot,

Without haste at the thick milling start;
This takes far more muscle than art;
It's not my mind; it's my heart;
    Ticker may tucker out.

Limp swung rope drops from jungle-gym tree,
Hangman knots to grip gingerly;
They make a monkey of me,
    Boy (emeritus) Scout.

Hold fast. Swing this deep rattlesnake ditch,
Barbed wire, palisado's steep pitch;
Straight run, abrupt reverse switch
    Primes (thump thump) the old pump.

Thorny brake, rocky creek, crumbly cliff:
Ankles twist, breath breaks, backbones stiff.
We'll make that final spurt if
    We take the water jump.

Machine-gun fire ahead. This *is* It.
Brave sound-effects: pop pop, pit pit.
Heads! No one aims to get hit
    Save some lunkhead ahead.

Bellies flat to the motherless dirt
Protect idiot or inexpert,
Yet this son's got himself hurt
    Or, as rumors run, dead.

Push on. He's past all maternal good.
He looks like Sarge said we all would.
Boom. It's a poor neighborhood.
    Pow. His body brews blood—

As we nudge him, brushing close by
Averting a shy craven eye,
Guessing we also may die
    Blotting up ruddy mud.

This, thank Christ, was the end of the race,
Each whole one saved his filthy face,
None tamed by outright disgrace
    Save the one with the wound.

What of his obese carcase? It bled;
Possessor played pompously dead.
Glimpsing his poor puréed head,
    Several stragglers swooned.

Sergeant glowed with legitimate joy;
This corpse was his cute plastic toy:
Hot air infused dummy boy.
    Blood was ketchup for real.

We've been cheated. Our hard triumph sours,
This excercise poor test of powers.
We can't claim courage as ours,
    Robbed of wounds that won't heal.

FIXER

Sol Factor was a fixer; it's very grateful I'm
To him, snatching from self-murder—me—marking penal time,
 Fourteen months stoking one stove from hot to cold.
  Sol Factor fixed me up, the punk,
With a flagrantly unexpected, still fragrantly recollected,
  Irrelevant, six-foot hunk
 Of Mormon gold.

One year, two months? A lifetime. Stir-crazy I've become.
I'm not lazy, Sarge; I lack a knack; nor am I playing dumb.
 Nightly I bank hot coals with my furtive pat;
  Hours before Sergeant's awake,
Scamper over, tamp her, fiddle her clinkers, diddle her damper,
  Give her a shiver and shake.
 She's out cold, flat.

"College fella? Jerk. What they teach you that there college?"
Anent this stubborn stove, naught but needless knowledge.
 "You've stuck here long enough. Can't you pull a wire?
  There must be some slot you can fill—
So be like me; go and see. Why, I'd try, I'd cry, I'd damn near die—
  Sure as hell I'd not lie still
 Friggin a fire."

Boing! A light goes me up—one frantic, prurient flame;
Filed among long unsavored names, one of well-favored fame—

Sol Factor, Pop's old pal from dank, stagnant Lynn.
     Like Dad, a lad with boundless gall,
Hutzpah (nerve); joins a ward-heeler's staff; coins his graft with cobweb craft;
     In trouble? Just go see Sol:
This Factor's *in.*

In what? South Boston's Dublin Club. Canny tactics, too:
Wid all dem shanty Oirish they could use one Yiddish Jew.
     Fixed bail double-quick in his bailiwick;
       Pulled the strings but spurned renown.
You want ice cut? Some crumb shut up, sprung, or fastidiously hung?
     Sol's the slickest trick in town
For kike or mick.

Time marches on. A war needs brains—Factor's not the least;
Washington's a kosher Barmecide's posh political feast.
     Sol's pitched his post in Old State-Navy-and-War.
       Lincoln's lank ghost, Wilson's grey shade—
Masters of lost American wars haunt these massive corridors.
     Sol's the Most. One's got it made
Once past his door.

"Whadja want?" Shark tooth, snake eye, fish flesh, skinned turtle nose.
Undone, I blushed in caitiff heat. Maiden sweat arose.
     "I heard you're here...." He blenched, betrayed: "So, and well?"
       "Pop just said to look you up, though
Everyone's here now, somehow, anyhow...." I know; I'd better blow.
     Snake eyes broil. Sol slurs: 'We'll go
To my hotel."

At the desk he claimed his key. A servile clerk inclined.

All Pow'r corrupts; abs'lute pow'r . . . I'm spineless, Lord; resigned,
    When wings from Heav'n, as if God's mind was in it,
        A mortal seraph, beauteous:

Burnished brass, blazing boots, snappy cap, tailored suit—he sure shoots
        The Works. Sol burps: "Excuse us,
    For a minute."

It's a warrant officer—strange rank, rare animal—

Interstitial, above us men, below the brass, yet all
    I've met incarnate their lonesome dignity.
        They prize their place. What's Buster's game?

Roughhewn jaw, suave supple lips, stropped blue chin, Choctaw tuft, belted hips
        Mean business. It's a shame
    He's not for me.

He's Factor's man, perquisite of egregious duty.

Sol's alarmed how hot I've got staring at blatant beauty.
    Comment's called for: "A guy I help now and then. . . ."
        I'll bet. Let's us three have a drink.

"No siree"—sternly—"Bill has his problems. I help lick 'em, fix 'em."
        Blinks his coy octipoid wink.
    Jay zus. Aye, men.

Upstairs, at least, real whisky. I'm starved, get fuzzy drunk.

No eats. Cheapskate. He wants me buzzed. o.k. God keep me, stunk.
    Nightmare exercise, the seamier side of war.
        Crut is dirt, so it tastes dirty

But grows absurd. We utter no word. Sol flutters, a girly bird.
        Time drags its ass. 10:30.
    Whoring's a bore.

Twin beds turned back; Fort Belvoir, long leagues away, by bus.
This bridal-suite's avid for the unlikely likes of us.
 Sol slinks to the john; hear his weak leak and hawk.
  I've missed my boat and lost my bet.
If I stay on, all else is lost. Grab the last of his liquor fast;
  Save my sacred honor—yet.
 I click his lock.

And make it! Lobby abandoned. Lone night-clerk, whilst there—
Ensconced in Morpheus' lap or an overstuffed easy chair—
 Lies Buster Bill snoozing, stupifiedly.
  Hah! Had Sol told him to return?
"Mister . . . " (Warrant officers aren't ranked "sir"; call him "mister ")
  "Don't sleep here"—since who shan't learn
 To swipe what's free.

Opal panther eyes peep ope in ripe astonishment:
Me, Sol's current trade, made so soon? He don't dig what it meant.
 "Bill"—man-to-man—"how about a hot square meal?"
  "You know a place?" We share the way.
Near by: The Shore Shack; straight rye, swordfish, pecan pie for a late dish.
  His move: "You got a place to stay?"
 "With you." It's real.

Hail Joseph Smith! Praise Brigham Young! Mormons bred my Bill;
An angel his ma, a saint his pa, winged from Cumorah Hill.
 Apostles schooled their corn sprout, ruled him thus:
  Gentiles shun their God-given sun;
Treasure pleasure it's due measure; the unusual's a refresher;
  Individuals: have fun,
 But make no fuss.

There's a Mormon hostel run for sainted servicemen.
The joint's shut; it's 2 a.m. Yet they let us in. So then
　　We shower, hit one soft sack—where, nothing loath,
　　　　Street-lamps pour florins o'er his chest.
Quoth Kit Marlowe: "I'll tell ye how smoothe his brest was & his bellie."
　　　　"Bless Sol Factor for this nest,"
　　Was what we quoth.

Bless Sol at sunrise (Sunday), a few more sunny days.
War plays its pawns in a funny madcap cat's-cradle maze,
　　Whence my sergeant charges in: "Hot news, kid!
　　　　You're shipping out, man. You know *when?*
Pronto. Chop-chop. *Overseas*. Now. Wow! Special Orders. Holy Cow!"
　　　　I didn't see Bill again.
　　Perhaps Sol did.

NEXT OF KIN

It's just one of those days,
Like the rest in their streaky, tiresome ways.
　　Young Bobby's been naughty so maybe, actually, he's sick;
　　He struck his sister, broke his wooden stick.
Grandpa agrees to take them off her neck for the afternoon.
They go. She prays they won't reappear soon.

The empty house, alone;
Interim breather for thoughts all her own

Untidily stacked like dishes slanting a full sink;
Tries to concentrate. She can't begin to think.
Glances at her mirror image. No startling beauty lurks there
To reassure an incurious stare.

Doorbell abruptly rings;
Answering, in her absent voice she sings
A tune she almost remembers; repeats its first phrase.
Walks unhurried towards the door in a daze.
Doorbell again; then again, again. What's your hurry (unworried).
Hurry, hurry; I will not be hurried.

Damn that stubborn bell.
The boy waits. Has he magazines to sell?
He seems overeager to hand her the thing in his hand.
She takes it, signs for it, hesitates, and
Goes back to the hall desk for some dimes or a quarter; finds one.
Slips him his tip. Thanks. The door clicks. That's done.

Telegram in light clasp;
Crumpled paper in her double-take grasp.
It's sheer nonsense. We regret to inform you, it said—
An odd practical joke—your husband is dead.
An attractive widow of thirty; two kids, one to be born;
Makes no sense feeling faint, lost, or forlorn.

Shrapnel? Flak? Leagues away
Spun through a shortened night to her whole day,
Wounding live weather to land hard on a bridebed here,
An infertile seedling to start a tear

Which only aborts. She begins to watch herself like a hawk:
I'm all right as long as I just don't talk.

Who puts cables in form?
She pictures wounded clerks, after a storm
    Of bloody murder compiling fractured lists, somehow;
    Names misspelled; error. No errors here, now.
His name correctly writ; her address undeniably right.
Permits her cautious mind its measure of fright.

Can she stand it or not?
She delays the decision, won't be caught
    In any reckless knot of hope or unfocused threats
    Recalling lucky or unlucky bets
On former stunning occasions. Surprise stabs, using his name:
Robert, Robert—mumbling shades of half-blame.

It's your fault, yours alone,
Robert—ending in an animal moan
    Which, thank God, none can hear. Still, what will become of me?
    Haste stoppers rank freshets of misery.
She'd best put his house in order. Her family comes home soon;
A dizzy neatness busies her immune.

Of course he had to go;
I know. I know. Stop it. He loved me. So
    Unkillable embers stir, warm on nothing at all
    Save firm throbbing echoes having no call
On valid faith or reliable prophecy, while of course,
It takes time to tame or disarm remorse.

Sensible girl she knows
She is. From now on, she'll have to get through
     As she can, her next day, week, month; years, one at a time;
     She, mild victim of his insolent crime
In getting killed. Clean house. Thank heaven for so tedious a task.
Bob! What was it like? Stop it. Never ask.

Proceed. Yes. And do it the
Quickest you can. Fix your face. She knows she
     Is better. Convalescence by forcing it couldn't
     Let feelings swell as they ought. Grief shouldn't
Spoil existence entire nor, indeed, should sorrow foretell
Her failure. The children ring her doorbell.

P. O. E.

This IS IT and so: so long.
     We're soldiers now, all set to sail.
We may not sing one sad old song
     Herded within a dark dock-rail.

Self-pity pools its furtive tear;
     Expect the Worst, discount the Best.
Insurance as a form of fear
     Tickles the terror in each chest.

So: THIS IS IT—yet not the sheer
    Crude crisis we've been trained to take,
For many a female volunteer
    Doles out thin cocoa with thick cake.

They've parked their limousines the while;
    Their natty uniform is spick
And span, their hairdo and their smile
    Pronounces patriotic chic;

And THIS IS IT for these dames too.
    We strive to fake a grateful note
But goddam duffel bag and pack,
    Gas mask, rifle, helmet, coat

Too heavy are, so each sad sack
    Must flop and gripe: This is *some* shit.
Up On Your Feet, our orders crack.
    It's All Aboard for THIS IS IT.

U. K.

CONVOY

Luxury liner "Britannia," mail carrier, 30,000 ton,
Once shipped sophomore and cardsharp to Le Hâvre and Southampton,
Hauling in happier season broker and buyer abroad,
Now transports monthly to battle thrice her tourist load.

"Britannia," rechristened "Alliance," altering former runs,
Was sunk first by Japanese claim, twice since by *untersee* Huns.
At 11:00 hours, 10,000 Yankees, black and white,
Cram each open inch of deck room, subway rush, sardine-can tight.

This enables seasick details to police up sleeping space
Stuffed in lounge, bar, kindergarten, cinema, or grand staircase.
At 12:00 ten loudspeakers, in accents hard to understand,
BBCeed from shores approaching, cough up news of war on land:

"Ah yew theah?" or "Cahn yew heah meh?" "Kerreh awn. Thet's awl foh naogh."
Theah King's English amplified heah mixes mirth from stern to bow.
Decks below, incipient tension tends to aggravate the scene;
Negro troops rip down the notice barring them a white latrine.

At 06:00 hours and at 16:00 too
In six shifts 10,000 swallow gooey beans in beany goo.
Above, in less congested quarters, brass chomps three shifts as it should:
Fruit cup, soup, steak, sweet, and coffee, off china, glass, and polished wood.

Then at 20:00, blackout. Every soldier should be sleeping
Or if not, then horizontal, place his soul in Captain's keeping.   **47**

Is my life preserver handy? Have I clothes in layers three?
Count knife, light, compass, candy, 'gainst the cold black open sea.

And with dawn, arises rumor: submarine just spied, or wreck.
Enemy plane near. Escort routed. Epidemic on D Deck.
Thus we roll through apprehension, weird malaise at every hand,
Till fresh white and black replacements stumble sea-legged onto land.

A PUB

Along rural British bypaths
    Rustic infants blond or sandy
Beg the GI: "Any gum, chum?"
    Answer is: "No candy, Andy."
At Bell & Bush, at Prince of Wales,
    At Bird in Hand or Bull & Bear,
Thirsty Yanks, we beg for Bitter,
    But there's no beer anywhere.
"Not a Drop" at George. From White Hart
    "Dry as Dust" we tikes our text
And the scrawl on Happy Dick's door:
    "Out of Beer till Thursday Next."

So we sprawls in public 'ouses
    Quaffing peppermint-and-gin
With released Eyetalian prisoners
    Who are pleased to be let in.

Some real wops with Yankee dagos
    Cop the taproom for their club,
Though the Home Guard in the backroom
    Feel put out of their own pub.
Comes the closing, nigh eleven;
    Doubled wartime's bright as day;
Farmer's been abed for hours
    While his lassies toss in hay.

As we pedal back to billet
    "Any gum, chum?" 's nighty-night.
"Not a stick, Dick" 's the wrong word now.
    "Gotta sister, mister?" 's right.

TEA

Embattled men of Britain
    Defend their native shore
Four long years, now nearly five—
    Bayeux to Bangalore.
These English needed allies;
    Their cousins came to aid.
With higher pay and better teeth
    Our coup de grâce is made.

English wives are widders
      Or we treats 'em much the sime;
Five years without an 'usband,
      It is a bloody shime.
A Yankee corporal's sitting
      In a dull provincial slum,
Upon his lap the son of a chap
      Who never seems to come.

It is true he may not,
      But then again, he may.
It's been so long it's really like
      Bert's always been away.
Corporal, himself an exile,
      Almost feels her a friend
Who puts her kid to cradle,
      Returns his blouse to mend.

It will not be forever;
      Orders are coming through.
We've just begun to whip the Hun;
      We'll need the corporal too.
Some time at last, presumably,
      Our corporal won't have gone;
He may be staying on to tea
      When Bert comes home.

Bert grasps the situation—
      After five long years,
Young Bertie in a Yankee's arms—
      And bursts into tears.

Bert will not try to kill him
　　As the corporal thinks he might:
He's had his fill of fighting;
　　He wants no fight.

He falters towards his teapot.
　　She offers him a scone.
They know this time tomorrow night
　　Each one will be alone.

EVENSONG

Though barely a believer,
　　It happened recently
My errant feet conducted me
　　Near sanctuary;
Not really to seek solace
　　Nor atone for sinful acts.
The noble meter in a prayer
　　Is what me most attracts.

Last night I went to Evensong;
　　The sun was at low tide.
Blown roses on a tower glowed
　　Like painted glass, inside.

One felt the tone of Jesu
    Was very seldom heard;
Parish and priest both mumbled
    His clearly uttered word.

But this was not significant:
    Far more impressive was
The domestic county feeling
    Of the curate for His cause.
He might have been a family friend
    Dropping by for tea,
Facing a cross, vaguely to ask
    Aid of some deity—

For King, country, and allies
    On land, at sea, in air;
Workers in factories or farms,
    Docks, mines, or anywhere
Their Imperial Ensign floats;
    For those we've hurt, for those we've lost—
Imprisoned, dead; for those we love;
    For those unloved who swell our host—

Thy mercy, Lord. That selfish roll
    Includes some villagers, a few
American enlisted men,
    Five aircraftsmen in tidy blue,
And me. All praise, thank, and rejoice
    Despite our bleak incurious eye,
Our absent automatic voice.
    Theirs and my humbling God is nigh.

TUDORESQUE

One adores the glory of England. When I was a scamp at school,
        The poet James Agee
And I listed the names of English kings, dates of their ev'ry rule—
        (Exeter's library);
Sketched coats-of-arms with sable bend and even a sinister bar,
        Baron or baronet;
We savored the fame of Tower jewel, Kohinoor and India's Star.
        Late afternoons we met
To devour the epic of England in ancient magazine views
        (Periodical stacks),
From leather-backed rusty volumes of the *Illustrated London News*.
        My first Shakespeare contacts
Were Jim's reading parts from the Histories aloud, fresh as current events.
        Favorite rôles were those
Of Bolingbroke, Hal, and Hotspur in bloody fine incidents
        Where bled the Tudor rose
Within the bosom of lover and friend: Prince Hamlet, Horatio.

        Often Hamlet was Jim;
We got drunk on Shakespeare's iambics and Britain's dynastic rainbow.
        I most remember him
Flipping the pages of portraits vignetted for the *London News*—
        The First War's English dead,
Glorious young men all, each a university graduate.
        Fate haloed every head,
All officers, baron or baronet, not one a mere private;
        History was alive.

Jim had such charm as Hamlet, I was happy Horatio, his friend,
      On four days out of five,
Though always I deem myself Denmark and shall play him to the end.

      At Harvard before long,
The casting is switched by Agee. He prepares the high comic schools,
      Sings us another song:
The chilly end of *Love's Labour's Lost* and *Twelfth Night*'s solemn fools,
      And Jim, setting forth strong,
Read me his own sug'red sonnets, which made noises like poetry
      Back then as they still do,
And Agee will dwell in English verse whilst, as for merely me,
      In footnotes I'll dwell too
For having first printed his verses in the quarterly *Hound & Horn*
      (A quote from Ezra Pound
Deeply revered in '26 before most Young Poets were born).
      Long since I've turned around;
I've had my fill of Fair Harvard, her Twentieth-Century Men;
      Theodore Spencer's dead
Who taught us the Age of Shakespeare, and his polymath Shakespeare then
      Was less of heart than head;
Our tutor was friend to Eliot, a ninteenth-century man
      From the seventeenth century,
So when we rewrote us our poems, the stanzas were wont to scan.

      What meant England to me
Apart from bards on Widener's shelves and Jim Agee's brandied voice?

      Britain: its earth, as well.
My people gave me a pilgrim's scrip, bade me make a scholar's choice: **54**

Tintagil's drear hotel—
Its Table Round of Morris fumed oak besprent with thumbed Debrett's;
Cathedral Close at Wells,
Where paddled a white-marble pride of swans with invisible coronets,
Tugged at the moat-house bells.

And I scaled the heights of Bloomsbury; I took rooms in Gordon Square.
I found some English friends.
At dazzling soirees, Lytton, Maynard, Clive, and Virginia were there.
Lydia superintends
Our *pas de deux*. Lopokova and I perform a world *première*
When I'm but sweet sixteen,
For the London seasons *entre les guerres* were Heaven and Vanity Fair,
The like since seldom seen.
At the head of St. James Street, silence. Crowds hush at brisk rattling brass:
The Household Cavalry.
An open coach thrones George the Fifth. From Paul's I see him pass:
"God bless Your Majesty!"
His mask salvaged from mortal ill, very model of some carved king.
He also is *my* king.

So here am I back in the ole U.K., endeavoring for to bring
Whatever decent thing
I can to repay my bad Yankee debts to English poesie.
It isn't hard at all.
England encourages allies with hearts and hearth, and I
Have billets within call
Of Third Army Headquarters, leased from a kind P.O. employee—
A Manchester suburb.
It's a tiny Tudoresque villa, but he's cleared a room for me;

The service is superb.
From Invasion Exercises I drag in bushed. Always, there he waits,
      Tea on his hob, and toast.
We prattle of the state of England and my own United States;
      We make our Allied boast
Of our present Grand Alliance and those futures we're fighting for.
      I tote him PX gum
For the brats of his son, at sea, who's actually winning this war;
      Splicing a brace of rum,
Since his boy's been absent from home five years, we drink deep to his luck—
      An *officer*, no less—
A tall fair youth with starry eyes, like Raleigh or Rupert Brooke
      (His snapshots show me this).
The *Illustrated London News* taught me that specific look
      From World War No. 1,
And declares my P.O. employee: Old England's come very far;
      Now, often things are done
Unthinkable thirty years ago when he'd fought a private's war:
      "Officer? Me? My eye!"
Yet look at his own Bertie now. And Bert's mother, at the door:
      "Daad, coöm ta baid." Hence I
Apologize for keeping him up. It's not that she hates us Yanks;
      She wishes we'd go home,
Though courteous as can be and decently renders her thanks,
      Yet I lack the aplomb
To make her love me for me myself or for my Amedican style:
      Intruder, and too fat.
She thinks I think this war's a lark and her suffering not worth while.
      Still, what she's getting at
Is part of a complex problem of country and class and taste

Useless to ponder on.
'Er 'usband disagrees. We're buddies, though our friendship be a waste,
        For soon it will be dawn,
Nearer that day I fare for France where wars are actually faced.

        We smother a sheepish yawn,
Ole Limey and young GI, hands-across-the-sea.

                                        I quit my foster home
        Shelved full of PX food,
To bivouac nights in a circus ground from the which I may not roam
        Unless I plan it good.
Our circus ground is guarded by fairly reliable MP's
        With itchy Tommy guns.
Often almost courageous, I've irrational fears of these
        Amongst some other ones
Mainly about a prepaid tour in a rational modern war
        Beyond this circus ground:
What lurks for Third (censored-dash-censored) Army, on foreign shore.
        Joe Sentry on his round
Lets nary a whisper drop on when we ship out or how we sail,
        But I'm not wholly lost.

I read in a week-old journal, th'invaluable *Daily Mail*,
        Snuck in here at some cost:
John Gielgud opens *Hamlet* in Manchester, right this selfsame week—
        Perchance this very night!
I start to charge batteries, low voltage of the terrible meek;
        Whether it's wrong or right,
John Gielgud I intend to view, granted Official Permission or not.

Of course it's bad to go;
Deserters from imminent invasions all deserve to be shot,
But I will see this show,
So I trickle out of our circus ground, nab a fast tram into town
As quick as you'd say "knife,"
And it *is* the Opening Night! My ticket costs me arf-a-crown—
The best night in my life
(In a theater). The house is packed; stuffed in a balcony sit
I, tight against a wall,
But knowing the words and the music and how the plot will fit,
I miss nothing at all
Of this greatest Hamlet of an epoch that saw Jack Barrymore.

My father, years ago,
Graded me all his Hamlets; awarded *grand prix* of princes for
Black Edwin Booth, although
He conceded Sir Henry Irving possessed the more argent voice.
Johnston Forbes-Robertson
(At least from photographs) had, until tonight, been my personal choice.

Soon is our drama done:
Ophelia (Peggy Ashcroft) was sideswiped by a flying bomb
Only two days before.
She goes daft with a bandaged wrist; her performance gains pow'r therefrom;
That's what Theater's *for*.
Gielgud beggars description; if its begetter could only have seen
His Hamlet to the life.
Our hearts are cleft in twain. He cradles, he cozens his mother-queen—
Minx, sister, mistress, wife.
No sweet prince ever drew breath dowered by dynasty or demesne,

Peer to his taffeta air,
His consonant hysteria, his generous insane
Cool canny candid stare
When he transfixes his schoolday chums, snapped links with a charmed lost youth—
Rosencrantz, Guildenstern.

But now this production assumes a superfetation of truth.
In my mind's eye still burn
That sunset end, that music at the close, that final scene of all,
That feast of corpses strewn:
(*Enter Fortinbras & British Ambassadors* . . .) We bite on breath:
Bright midnight on black noon.
(*Drums, colours, attendants* . . .): "This quarry cries on havoc. O proud Death...."

What did those English find?
An empty throne (*stage center*). Loyal Horatio at post, on guard,
Nor has he lost his mind—
Snatches the crown from his bleeding prince, ill-starred and starry eyed.
He sets that hollow crown
Upon its seige imperial. Hail! The king lives nor ever has died.
Then kneels Fortinbras down,
And this piece is no longer Gielgud's nor is it Shakespeare's either,
Though both make all come true.
It blazons the armour of England in every sort of weather:
Treason or buzz bomb too.
England shares actor and poet with soldier, civilian, and all
Allies, of whom I'm one.
England, what thou wert, thou art. Bang hands. Roar throats. Teary curtain call.
Thus all her wars are won.

BOY SCOUT

Above a target harbor in the wood of a private park
Cowers our marshaling area 'neath its pre-invasion dark;
    No pinpoint matchstrike warns the sky where our alerted armies wait
    The long expected last command to ship us to our drastic fate.

A youth from Sacremento gags, throbbing in his tongue-tied fright:
"I have so much to live for still," sweating it into Hampshire night,
    South of that "Southern England" where buzz bombs drone and fall.
    "We have so much to live for still" is sincerely echoed by all
His buddies, noncoms, officers—some fazed but most of whom won't budge,
Including medics and nurses who, in a blacked-out tent, boil luscious fudge.

Our Sacremento soldier leans on a nubile tree,
Extracts an ancient Scout knife to carve initials three:
    "I'll brand my name on England deep in this sapling tall;
    Until this sapling wax to wood, in France I shall not fall."

His glance above at its branches discovers the treetop is dying;
His heart contracts at the omen, but instinct, death-defying,
    Hunts him an older stouter trunk, a Robin Hooded bolt of oak
    To hack his three initials deep with an Eagle Scout's unflinching stroke:
"My name shall live forever," though as he finishes
Feels the next bright buzz bomb burst in a field beyond these trees.

JUNIOR

Junior had his hair cut the night before we sailed;
Barber cropped his childish skull as if he'd just been jailed.
When we dragged up the gangplank I was ten feet behind
And saw his shiny nob ahead, so kept him in my mind.

I knew we all were wary, a few quite terrified,
But I'd *my* fears to foster and needed none beside.
Our crew of merchant seamen gaily prepared our boat;
We soldiers marked their easy way and envied them their lot.

Fog floated in and found us. We lost all ships around.
Our danger was collision unless we ran aground.
Also there were submarines waiting for it to clear—
Torpedo boat and strafing plane and floating mine to fear.

I heard a merchant seaman no longer laugh. He cursed:
"Of all my forty crossings, tonight's the very worst."
Thus we knew THIS WAS IT again and wished to Christ that we
Were safe at home or snug abed beyond the mortal sea.

Then Junior, through our nightmare, came stalking quick but dead;
As I absorbed his fright from him, the mist on his shaved head
Stood out like sweat. His two wild paws in helpless animal fright
Trapped me in the clamp of love to nurse him through this night.

He was in peril. So was I. Be with us to the end
Where every selfish soldier is rationed half a friend.

France

BLACK JOE

This Norman coastal meadow lies in a chill grey haze of light;
A soldier first sees France by day; he'd hit the beach at night.

Stepping over snoring men, he tries to find him fire;
Uncle Tom cooks for Uncle Sam as once he had for hire.

Our soldier thanks the happy black, returns to his own group,
And from those borrowed embers brought, a sharp new flame flares up.

One by one his drowsy gang uncoils from each stern bed,
Stiffens to stretch, scratch, realize not one of them is dead.

Around our fire, like bugs to light, amble a few dazed oxenstray
Negro troops who've slogged all night, orchard from beachhead, miles away.

We whites, with gummy eye, but brave, as our blond blood stirs to its round
Stare hard the dark intruders down to stand our own usurpèd ground.

With psyches sound, but half-awake, we keep possession of our pyre,
Warding the somber soldiers off; this shall remain a white-man's fire.

Thus hard arrayed, fright against fright, upon the first dawn of our fight
In common against a common foe, smoulders their wrong against our right.

BED CHECK

Everyone's a wee bit nicer if we sniff some danger nigh,
Kindlier to one another when we think we're going to die.

Sleep is scarcely absolution; by half-past one or two
Their engines hum; our ack-ack barks; an enemy is needling through.

A drumbeat detonation of their cannonading drum
Spits out machine-made murder to startle every chum.

We feel the sinister low drone of Jerry—deeper than our planes'—
And sense him circle low to take a dose of tracer for his pains.

Should we haul on our helmet or roll in our foxhole?
I nudge my moron tentmate. How best to save the soul?

He mumbles for a moment, shoves over with a sigh,
Grumbling it's immaterial whether we live or die.

So I shake him: "Listen, Buddy; Bed-Check Charlie's overhead;
We had better take to cover or risk the falling lead."

Then Bud and me, we shudder, our rancor half forgot,
To hear the Jerry plane buzz off, goosed by a parting shot—

Laid out like lovers, tense but tamed, coupled within sin's droll device,
Worried and married, damp and lame, to let our pauper hearts de-ice.

A VET

A tired new trooper scans the beach
   Where but some twenty dawns before
He, with those thousands of his force,
   Barely achieved this shallow shore.

Through hip-high water over flats
   Gritty cross fire cracked its knife;
Aching blasts sucked all the air
   From quick collapsing sacks of life.

Here where near-misses lapped his craft
   Landings by dozens scar the sand;
There where scratched-off bombers plunged
   Beetle-boats swarm the busy strand.

Across the bay, blunt puffs of smoke;
   A war seems somewhere—miles from here.
He feels its desultory bang:
   Land mines blown by engineers.

Just three weeks after our great act
   He can't recall half his own wild
Sobbing advance. High on a dune,
   This prematurely aging child,

A mite of history he helped make,
   Rubs stubble chin, and spends a sigh.
Tomorrow he'll be down the line
   Waiting one more chance to die.

TENT-MATES

It's no cinch to live together
　　In a field three acres square
With your noncoms and your officers
　　Sleeping and eating there.
Soldiers aren't chosen wisely
　　To be four-season friends;
Neither lovers nor companions,
　　We were picked for rougher ends.
Hence our interest seems to lessen
　　In snapshots of buddies' wives,
Nor are we all-absorbed by
　　Incidents in lurid lives
Which startlingly resemble
　　Our own grim or comic tale
But which, on other lips than ours,
　　In passion tend to pale.
From living in each other's laps,
　　From sniffing at each other's pores,
From glimpsing every function of
　　The human mechanism's chores,
From dozing next to unloved flesh,
　　From swimming in the common stew,
We're trigger happy to the touch
　　At our compulsive rendezvous.
I do not mind my own shit.
　　Why then avoid another's?
Answers are articles of war:
　　Men are seldom brothers.

LA GRANGE

This farm is France entire, in peacetime as in war;
Its order and its amplitude, now as ever before:

The house, more grand than farmhouse; its yard more court- than farm-;
Its peeled pink crust of plaster—pale, flaky, fresh-loaf warm;

The pear espaliered on old brick—complete: farm, garden, manse—
The frugal elegance of man, all that is best of France

Has been within the last four years invaded from both east and west.
The Germans killed the bulls and boys, and now we Yanks condemn the rest.

We sad sacks don't think much of France; it's rainy, poor, and cold.
The cider tastes like vinegar and all the girls are old.

This farmer waters cattle; his good wife scrubs her pan;
How dare they, shod in wooden shoon, deem us barbarian?

We dial our radio on New York and, hypnotized, all but forget
The state of war, the facts of life; the dirt, the distance, and the wet.

A cow, two years unserviced, blood burning, makes her choice:
She mounts a sister. We stare rapt. Jazz lends its Technicolor voice.

"I'll be goddamned," a Bronx boy vows, who's heard his pa report this place:
"Them frogs certainly seem to be a queer preverted type of race."

The frustrate cow slides off her mate; the silly pair rejoin their troupe.
The farmer comes to call his kine. His wife rubs garlic in her soup.

The Bronx boy and his hungry chums flow chow-wards with vast appetite:
Dried Klim, canned butter cellophaned, a bite-sized feastlet packaged right. **69**

RED CROSS

Come, fellas, all: react with glee. A special treat's in store today.
At half past nine, peculiar time, the Red Cross will a visit pay.
   We are not wounded; no, nor slain; but there's real pain in every breast:
   We're filthy homesick and we crave the cushion of a female chest.

The Red Cross operates a van endowed by Kohn's Department Store,
Equipped with hot plate, radio, and society virgins three or four.
   Our CO sniggered when he said we'd best change shirts and scrape our chins,
   And even officers are glimpsed abluting shyly, trim as pins.

Three girlies aren't much use to our three acres of gaunt GI's,
But what the hell, we'll have a smell: any can win a sweepstake prize.
   So hear the dulcet strains of jazz. Their truck has rolled onto our ground;
   A long queue swiftly sweeps its tail our ladyless encampment 'round.

Standing in line, three hundred joes grin boylike and self-consciously,
Nudging the quicker ones ahead step up for doughnut and coffee.
   Doughnuts are tender cakes with holes which Yankee maids of standards pure
   Substitute symbolically for many acts they mayn't endure.

Doughnuts are token too of home, and coffee also, cool and weak,
And here am I to pour my pint and sight them knockers, lips, and cheek.
   Pat, the svelte cute Redcrosstitute has left Lake Forest far to heel;
   Mechanic, stainless steel intact; sisterly, wholly unreal:

"Now, soldier, where do you hail from? Utah Dakota well that's fine
Step lively please we've lots to serve you're all too sweet the war's divine." **70**

Yet her efficient insincere hard-boiled charm and stenciled smile
Are quite undone by her machine; for, honestly, we're touched the while

That radio bass-baritone incanting o'er her doughnut stove
Sings innocently "Water Boy," making us all think thoughts of love—
Of mother, mistress, kiddy, wife; melting each eye by simple song:
"Jack O'Diamonds, Water Boy . . ." sobs home is far as war is long.

AWOL

Three shots sting our resounding night; three scattered shots. Then all is still.
Dreamers raise their heads from bed—at what alarm, attack, or kill?
Listen again: no sound at all, save a roused cock in a barnyard
Or convoys pouring down the pike. Roll back to sleep. Men stand our guard.

By morning we learned who shot what: a Texan combat engineer
Pounding our points for seven weeks mixed feral fright with frisky fear.
Finally something has to snap. A bottle full the fellow finds,
An empty jeep, roads to the rear; from this man's army he resigns.

His joy ride dumps him in a ditch. Our drunken craven lands him hard;
Arises, cracks his piece three times; bumps into our alerted guard.
Sentries with ready weapons drawn advance on him as toward a foe,
Back him against a barnyard wall while some are glad to see him so.

An officer comes to command, arranges his correct arrest
Paternally and patiently as if it all is for the best.

Grins our deserter: "Thank you, sir. Was I scared pissless! Now I'm great.
Give me a break, boss. Call my base. It's Lucky Conqueror 468."

Whether he did we never knew, and later no one seemed to care;
A guy told me who'd been on guard and seen this soldier sweating there
Badgered by some bully boys whom battle had not bit till then,
Their trigger fingers itching in conceit they too were veteran.

Courts-martial grade delinquency as frantic terror plus strong drink.
Cowardice? No; hysteria. Heroes recover in the clink.

S CHIMBLY

So it is the Cotentin Peninsula middle July 1944
When took place unusual incidents of our great second world war.
Of them the first time it is I tell now at full length
Result of overemphasis of military strength.

The date is late afternoon on a Friday warm and fair
Major William S. J. Dabeney is the officer in charge there.
This character is known often as Silly Willy to his men
In energy and efficiency a fine civilian specimen.

His unit has its orders U.S. Civil Affairs Unit C34(b)
Trained to take over all town management in all Germany
When Germany is all overtook then seems a long way off
An event at times we laugh our heads off to scoff.

Fact is, Jerry (as we call all them enemy Huns right then)
A last desperate stand he makes Cherbug right acrost to KN
We are midway waiting something good for it to break
Having nothing to do Dabeney didn't want our morale to slake.

Major W. S. J. Dabeney USCAU C34(b) our company did command
The vim and vigor he makes us in every way demonstrate is grand.
Before this he was town manager in some old Mississippi town
A sanitary engineer he come in with fame and renown.

Dabeney he figger busy fingers keep us outta pecks a trouble
Often sounding off you all come here men on the double.
At first at his enthusiasm we poke considerable fun
But in time fine out he is sure one son of a gun.

He pitch his tent we sleep puptents then on orchard ground
Nice set up with invention and appliances his area did abound.
We build him duck-board floor and slat wooden bedstead
Painting railings around his cot blue white and fire-house red.

He insist strict cleanliness good policy all times to pursue
He organize our pipe system two punched cans on us all to spew
Hot and running cold water with deep drain down rock and earth
Enjoying hot and cold water showers was to us often much worth.

We dig up wild flowers and stick them each in painted pots
Ornamenting our medic tent where we go get shot our shots.
All pretty and nice as nice and pretty can be
To set up some new project took lots of ingeneuity.

Dabeney hopes to construct a fireplace in summer warm
At first a fireplace middle July seemed not too much harm?
Nevertheless we got no fire brick our immediate area
So some fellows and me we exappropriate a medium weapons carrier.

We tear down past old Isigny too past old Carentan
In front an old church where must of been wunst a front lawn
A fair size brick pile of smooth brown grey beauty
To liberate this here pile of brick become our immediate duty.

Dabeney due to several delays he become ornery and mean
We hope his temper improve wunst this excellent brick he seen.
This way it work out he grins and is very glad
And tells us men erect a tall chimbly no more sore or sad.

Them bricks are nice in the hand well made and smooth
Perfect surface and edge smelly faintly of spice or clove?
A few crumbles most baked hard lays out nice and firm
All are eager to light fire in this chimbly and watch it burn.

We don't wait long sunny July temperature is very fine
Sun sets. Movies after chow where we all stand in line.
Major Dabeney sticks around to try his new falicity
Only one left behind to test it with himself was he.

I forget the name this film. It had been good I'd remember it.
Colossal explosion. Brother. Jerry finally got us all hit?
We gallop up where bright fire flame and screaming sound
Old Silly Willy knocked out cold on the hard ground.

Lucky he isn't hurt worse. Minor cuts and bruises
When he comes to all medical aid he bravely now refuses.
He wants to get back to his fireplace staggers up there
He look at that big hole and stare and stare and stare.

Colonel comes up. "Say Major why are you standing there?"
Dabeney answers "Sir a mystery is here I declare
I light my perfect fireplace it blew sky high.
Miracle many personnel and I didn't actually die."

Colonel looked peculiar at Silly Bill shaking his head
He picking up bitty brick bits offen the ground and said
"Major Dabeney I swear you are smart and right bright
How come build chimbly out of abandoned Jerry dynamite?"

INTER-SERVICE

September morn in Norman June: slack sag of middle age in folds;
A comfy tum, a flabby bum refreshed by wet, astringent cold.
Behold our British officer. For forty years he's briskly passed
From town- to country-house to hunt, yet bathes before he breaks his fast.

Even upon this rawbone dawn when brass revelly boasts no sun
Espy him sluice his tingling buff; long e'er we're up, his douche is done.
On rosy, prickling epiderm th' Anglican offertory's spilt.
How he ablutes and scrubs his roots! It is his prime, imperial guilt.

Thus did he douse on Khyber Hill amid a border station's rocks,
Rinsing the taint of hard-set caste, pulled on a pair of clean white socks.
With mineral waters cleansed himself despite the Blue Nile's fetid stain
And sponged away fellahin clay sullied by pharaoh's rotten strain.

Staunch as pounds sterling, all awash, his skin keeps fresh in ambience foul;
Around his world the Union Jack has served as pup tent and as towel.
He's bid our Bud to light his fire.   Bud's no mere batman born to be;
He orders me to boil him tea, which in our ranks ain't s.o.p.

He does not dig us Yanks as yet; stout fellas, aye; but rude, but odd.
Whose big idea has hauled him here to boss our unit, poor old sod?
On paper, Ike's plan looked real great: one-half of us, enlisted men
With British officers; at Caen, there, English own Amediken

Officers. We bet they're snafu too. Well—every trick we gotta try,
Though such arcane experiment is doubtless doomed to early die.
Such coils made us wage wars before, o'er Common Sense, Tea Party too,
And 1812. Hence, here we are, wondering, at Caen, who's fooling who.

'Is Lordship's at 'is ruddy ole rub, prize product of the Public School.
We are not serfs claim Bud and I, beneath British colonial rule.

2

So what? So he's a Scotsman born and bathes each dawn, a marvel rare.
Thrice he's cadged water from our fire; today we caught him ling'ring there—
Enemy, ally, and at once, gentleman, alien, officer.
Puir dog-fices, we keeps our plice, repelling him with curt snapped "Sir."

A pity. He needs room to think; begs pardon for the place he took;
We scarce can credit our sharp eyes when we behold his precious book.   **76**

In our vexation we ignore, though Britain share our General Staff,
She's enlisted Chaucer's weather, Hamlet's humors, Falstaff's laugh.

England condemned my boyhood gods; gave Wilde a gaol, Byron exile;
Owen, David Jones, Sassoon, honored their General Staffs in style.
Indignant verses mayn't absolve the snob, the tyrant, or the fool,
But, peace or war, when foolish games the snob ordains by tyrant rule,

British poets have always purged the curse of class or pride of purse.
Pardon the sponge bath. Thank God for the Oxford Book of English Verse.

CHATEAU

France, our enchantress, Europa's ripest daughter,
Waits wide-eyed, trembling over bloodied water.
Among French ladies, and the least unripe,
A restless widow stars as prototype
Of classic womanhood, drowsy or waking,
Apprehensive of our huge undertaking.
Kindled by swarming low-flown glider planes,
Chilly in her big bed, she tries to sleep again.
Woman in war, full blown, loveless, alone,
A recluse throbbing in a combat zone,
She keeps one maid, more comrade than a slave,
Lower by birth but every whit as brave—
Cheerful, ingenious, constant Marguerite
Swallows what's bitter, savors all the sweet.

Captain Rick Adams holds in his command—
Bodyguard, chauffeur, and staunch right hand,
Not one to worry, gay at savage game—
Salvator Bardi is this esquire's name.
He takes his young captain in easy stride,
Steers each catastrophe a smoother ride;
Breasting the wars in frolic haziness,
Peasant sagacity condones some laziness.
"Adams—" he figures, "poor bastard's nervous,
Lacking a central aptness for our service.
There's something specious in his public stance;
He's got the willies. Give the guy a chance.
Heroic soldiering's his masquerade;
What that lad needs is just to get him laid."

Both have bit battle: bog-oak's splintered roots
Rear snap-haft trunks to harvest parachutes:
Harness fouled, vast lustrous silks stained red
With all unchampioned jumpers dangling dead.
They spot their target drop from dubious maps;
Landmarks switch, shrink, vanish. Perhaps
They're lost or luckless—what to judge it by?
Waiting on reinforcement from the sky . . .
Six Jerry tanks roll up and wipe them out—
All save Adams and Bardi, his smart scout. . . .
Our beaches build. They find a stranded jeep,
In which this precious pair fresh vict'ries reap.
Prospecting possible command-post sites, they go
Straight up the *allée* of her trim château.

Tires crunch a grass-grown court; Adams hops down.
Framed by her portal, in an old tea-gown,
A Norman lady; by her, Marguerite:
Twin anxious welcomes sneaky Yankees greet
Who would pre-empt this house.　Shut, rigid, shy,
Captain averts his sly appraising eye.
Mistress routes them through room on room,
Pausing in salon to enumerate heirloom—
Portrait bust, Gobelin, sunburst chandelier:
A race of gentlefolk held high state here.
Captain confesses to the valor of a louse:
Has he got guts enough to commandeer her house?
Mere social visit should have been a raid;
His sergeant lags behind to date the maid.

Champagne erupts, a sacramental drink.
Adams may touch no drop but marks Sal Bardi wink:
Refusal is unmannerly, might muster trouble.
Protestant lips boggle on popping bubble.
Missing no hint, the countess plies his cup,
Whilst Richard, getting giddy, laps it up.
Things are going great, if too damn quick:
Sergeant Bardi won't want his captain sick.
Better get cracking—Isigny, miles away—
A good beginning—let's call this a day.
Little is mentioned of headquarters' claim;
Contact's been made. Four hearts beat each the same—
In principle. Provocative farewell—
Captain to countess; sergeant, mam'selle.

2

Americans recross the glimmering *bocage*,
Advancing towards imminent Marivauxdage.
Adams must gain his leasehold on her place
By main compulsion, though he'll strive for grace.
Bardi withdraws, beckoned by Marguerite;
They launch a brave campaign on armagnac, neat.
Captain has plans no woman may defer;
He shall be masterful, but can he count on her?
Her bed reiterates it could comfort two
If she'll teach him the least of what to do.
He takes experiment for scientific investigation,
No worse than a thorough physical examination.
She plays night nurse—or, rather, little sister.
Our rascal might, just for kicks, have kissed her.

Rick, our avenging angel, bison from the sea,
Foam-flecked, flame-licked in nude theophany,
Offers stark solos of flirtatious fun
To spike all hints of rapine unbegun;
Gauging handstands before her small log fire—
Flexed flank, abdomen—tan suede on copper wire—
Sports every flashy caper in the book.
A misfired backflip crystal pendants shook.
She stares amazed, amused at such charade,
His transfixed public. Now must he parade
Somersault, cartwheel. Had there only been,
Replacing oak parquet, a springboard trampoline!...

None's needed: moist with flushed aromatic roses,
Upon her cozy hearth the sweaty idiot dozes.

She too's quite conquered by his cabaret—
La fille de Minos et de Pasiphäe—
Outraged Europa by a bullock daunted.
His heifer breathing, measured insult, taunted
A widow wiser than this wastrel's mother,
Nor can she compare him with any other
Lover. Phaedra is prophetess. He's stormed her shore
Risking stupendous parts to win her war,
Yet wants too little. She concedes defeat;
But who's won what? Ungenerous retreat
Of victor vanquished. Can this churlish boy
Be freed to treat the world as his new toy?
She strokes his milky virtue like a pet.
A man-size dreamer nuzzles vain regret.

AIR STRIKE

This was the morning to recall: steep azure, stunning, diamond-bright,
An empty cloudless bell-clear shell, stupendous scale for such a sight.
We groundlings held our bivouac field, the ordinary work in hand,
Protected by a pasture plot, busy and far from battle land.

Abruptly up from out our west, heralded by a droning hive,
Swept over level throbbing air, the stinging squadrons, death alive.

Hand upon hip in proud amaze, soldiers dropped hatchet, nail, and saw:
Four thousand planes roared overhead. We all were speechless in our awe
Of Yaveh, Thunderer, Battle God, who in His just, avenging wrath
Hath lent us much matériel bigger and better than Jerry hath.

This mathematic vision showed four thousand planes complete with crew,
Servant mechanics back at base, whilst over oceans, not a few
Tinkers who'd tooled, sailors who'd shipped, these marvels matchless oversea.
Conceive the method and the mind controlling such dread formulae.

To many, it meant money spent; to others, some vague Bad or Good,
Trying to render in tight terms the vast logistics as we could.
An amateur, I multiplied my balance of equivalents,
How I would handle so much cash, or bad, or good, and how events
Always propel hectic techniques to end up in the hands of those
Who ever manfully insist on any program save repose.

In any case, four thousand planes flew overhead and we were there.
That night, we listened for the news. It was not mentioned on the air,
But at the morrow's trumpet-sun, the big guns sounded strong and slow.
We'd cracked their salient, and we were some kilometers past St. Lô.

HIJACK

We drive all day from mildly picturesque Coumbes-sur-Seine
Through impressionist landscape it's nice to be seeing again;
My colonel, no companion of choice, uncorks his private pint of pain.

I've driven for this old pre-World-War-I crock before.
He doesn't like me for stink; I deem him a snobby old bore;
But we're inextricably linked by certain tensions ingrained in this war.

His grief derives from a grandson he's crazy about
Whom he's learned was captured two days ago in a censored rout
Of U.S. troops. Now we ride up front fast trying to find something out.

North, ever north; then northeast. Disturbing tableaux abound—
Relics of men and machinery, busted husks tossed around.
As we roll through sinister buzzings, nervous-making mysterious sound

Upsets us and—bang—we stall in a small market square—
But how best to describe it? A pitched battle takes place right there
While the parties engaged wear one uniform: ours. Interpret this scare

As some insane gag, but now a big gasoline truck
Overturns. Jerry-cans bounce on fierce combatants striking or struck
By fist, gun butt, monkey wrench. If we have only average luck

Things won't pop, someone get hurt: us. I watch Colonel stand
In our dead jeep shouting orders, though none obey his command
Sensible as it sounds: "Stop, boys; stop right now," and then his good right hand

Reaches for side arms. I yank him down, jerk our jeep back.
Bodies swivel around the vehicle and dusk dyes to deep black
While it all gets more unreal although staying real enough. Absolute lack

Of discipline or authority. Colonel slumps down
Sulking through this crazy vague riot in a French border town
Where American soldiers sock one another for some obscure renown.

Hence: construe this authentic hilarious scene,
Melodramatic yet stereoscopic. What has just been
Logical chaos stems from hysteria mainly about gasoline.

Our motorized units forged so wildly far ahead
Many imagined they'd seized victory but were then stopped dead.
Whichever eager beaver planned this mad push should have stood in bed.

Hence we hijack gas from whom gas has to hijack;
There's nowhere near enough to make up our present serious lack,
Not alone to sustain an advance but to stop being shoved way back.

Colonel and I, in sort of a bad spot, are safe enough.
I still have, thank Christ, my own tank half full of the sacred stuff,
Which brings us back to base though driving blackout routes by night is rough.

My pre-World-War-I officer sweats in the dirt
Clinging to a great American army losing its lousy shirt—
His adored grandson captured by the enemy; lost, maybe hurt. . . .

PATTON

Skirting a scrub-pine forest there's a scent of snow in air;
Scattered sentries in smart combat dress accord us their sharp stare;
My chaplain for the first time now allows as where we are:
      At the core of this campaign.

Detroit's vast ingenuity subsumes our plans for doom,
Commandeers an auto-trailer to serve as a map-room;
Hermetic and impersonal, one may reasonably assume
      This is Third Army's brain.

I spy a female nurse pass by, baiting a white bull-pup,
Official pet of General's and a humane cover-up
For isolated living or affection's leaky cup
      At secret headquarters.

Nurse accepts my chaplain's solemn amateur salute;
He lets the pup lick and sniff his shiny combat boot,
Shoots her a semiprecious smile which all agree is cute—
      Raps on that map-room door.

Should I from sloppy jeep jump out and to attention snap?
Patton's informal entrance seems some sort of booby trap,
But his easy stoic manner is devoid of any crap,
      So I stick right in my car.

Measuring our morality or elegance in war,
I marked our nurse compose herself. Starch-white, she primly wore
A gold-filled heart-shaped locket on her chest, and this was for
      Second, minute, hour.

Time's analysis is portable and only time can tell
What's in the works for all of us—nurse, chaplain, general.
Syllables in seperate hour, minute, second, simply spell
          Military power.

Our brass cut short their conference, and Patton turns to me:
"Well, soldier, how about a cup of hot delicious tea?
Unless I am mistaken, Nurse may even add whisky."
          "Oh, thank you, sir," I said.

"Chaplain says you come from Boston. Then you know it is my home;
Now both of us are many miles from Bulfinch's golden dome.
By springtime it is where I hope the both of us may come
          Provided we ain't dead."

Nurse's watch ticked its temporal tune. Chaplain and I returned
To our base of operations whilst vict'ries blazed and burned.
Reckless Patton's vehicle one year later overturned:
          I see him as a saint.

Angels who flanked his final fling to martial glory's niche
Named Lucifer as honor guard, for that son of a bitch
My immortal captain's mortal, and also he touched pitch;
          His stars tarnished from taint.

In *Stars & Stripes* we read it when he slapped that soldier down
Cringing in a psycho-ward to play the coward clown,
Presuming to a state of shock (he'd smashed a stubborn town),
          But Patton blew his stack.

For me and my companions whom slap and shock stung too
Though minimal responsible find other factors true:

The pathos in enlisted men's not special to the few;
          It is the generals' lack.

Inspecting cots of amputees, unshaken obviously,
Approves the stitch above the wrist, the slice below the knee;
Hides in th' enlisted men's latrine so he can quietly
          Have one good hearty cry.

This soldier has to take a leak, finds someone sobbing there.
To my horror it's an officer; his stars make this quite clear.
I gasp: "Oh, sir; are you all right?" Patton grumbles: "Fair.
          Something's in my eye."

With vict'ry's brittle climax pity's never far away;
Patton feels only wounds should hurt which help him win the day.
But wounds have casual exits and it's often hard to say
          If blood flows in or out.

When endowed as a fine artist you can fling the paint around;
Or, called to seek salvation, you can make a solemn sound.
But crafty priestlike soldiers keep one premise as their ground:
          Loose fright ends up as rout.

Patton's a combat artist; hence his palette runs to red;
Makes superior generals anxious he's prone to lose his head,
Spoil pretty Rhenish landscapes with an April coat of lead:
          Our man may go too far.

The British and Canadians are ordered to push through;
Patton learns he's just their anchor with nothing much to do
But cultivate impatience, curse and sweat or curse and stew—
          Not his concept of war.

He vows: "Now you go fuck yourselves. I'm taking off from here."
He vanishes, nor hide nor hair. At SHAEF there is grave fear.
They bid him halt; he wires 'em straight: "I HAVE JUST TAKEN TRIER,
        SO SHALL I GIVE IT BACK?"

Military governor, Bavaria's shattered state,
He had a naïve notion which was not so all-fired great;
Hired him all former Nazis who'd nicely coöperate.
        For this he gets the sack.

And yet—it's not entirely fair. Since war is done and won,
Patton fears peace as idleness, peacetime as seldom fun;
Idleness is devil's business, and for the devil's son
        Good Nazis don't rank least.

This old pro was an innocent. Thank Christ for simple souls,
Pearl pistol-packin' poppa, prince of polo's thousand goals,
And I'm not fooling you, my friend: he starred three major rôles:
        Warrior, craftsman, priest.

We were rained right out of Nancy. Firm Metz we could not free.
Floods muddied fields; his bogged-down tanks less use than cavalry;
Came his orders: ALL PERSONNEL WILL PRAY THAT THESE UNSEA-
        SONABLE RAINS SHALL CEASE.

George Patton through proper channels forwards his request.
There comes logical reply to logistical behest;
Who am I to testify it's some joker's sorry jest?
        Rains cease. His tanks make peace.

SPY

They don't reveal the whole deal. You proceed without clue.
Sometimes I can guess, but more often not.
The duty is: Drive straight, keep your trap shut,
Pretend you're not present, get 'em there. But
It's hard to act dumb knowing someone's got to be shot.

Eavesdropping helps, so today I deciphered it through
The tense stance of official reporters
Detailed to observe the last throes of those
Whom gallantry tempted, recklessness froze
To a wall at the rear of Third Army Headquarters.

I was assigned a prize committee from our G2:
Colonel, in real life a lawyer of weight;
Major, a fatty at home in his bank;
Chaplain, an athlete whose fair hair and frank
Grin made me happy to drive for him early or late.

To the stockade I drove them, set them down with relief,
Parked in the staff motorpool right behind,
Checked with Motor Sergeant, a man I knew,
Hung on, trying to pry hints from him too.
No soap; waiting, turned off my motor, turned on my mind.

Soon they emerged. Which mask betrayed personal grief?
Slumped in their seats none seemed eager to go—
Where? Nowhere, anywhere; back to home base. . . .
I strove to deduce from every shut face
What all had been shown. Not a one would easily show.

Colonel Law said: "You'll admit he had a fair trial."
Sighed Major Gold: "It's the price to be paid."
Chaplain: "He certainly was a brave lad."
Smiling, stared hard at me, truly sad:
"Right to the end yet never the least bit afraid."

Did he fall crying Heil Hitler or Deutschland Heil?
Fanatic student or patriot brute?
What meager disguise had we trapped him in?
I saw me, his unidentical twin
But unable to muster a similar salute.

A spy judged and shot kept us worried mile after mile.
His busy echo blurred its short breath.
Was there one thing we'd die for as he had—
Land, leader, any notion—good or bad?
What was worth it? Were we all, then, unworthy of death?

INTERPRETER

In her cold, unlighted piece
    Six flights above the street
She's pinned by us inquisitors
    Who brutally repeat
Questions she's already sworn
    Answers she doesn't know.
But that was to their dull police
    While we are different, though

We have our style of charm quite like
    Her friend, a Francophile;
Both of us are generous
    With cigarette and guile.
My captain speaks no French. He feels
    Futile in his distress;
He formulates a foolish trap
    Which even he must guess
May never net so sly a doe:
    "Ask her," he orders me,
"Was she—intimate—with this joe?"
    And she: "What's intimacy?"
"Well, did she have—goddam it, man—
    Relations with this kid?"
"*Bien. Relations . . . on peut dire.*"
    So try again we did.
"If what you mean is what I think"—
    She frowns; her cigarette
Has smouldered out and she won't ask
    For another one just yet—
"Why, yes. He's sweet. I like him well.
    And what is wrong with that?"
Stretches, yawns, purrs, spreads herself
    To curl, a svelte house-cat.
Commands my captain: "Ask her more,"
    But senses his defeat,
So after further feeble jabs
    We issue to the street.
My captain never will confide
    In this enlisted dough;

Aside from rude conjecture I
   May never really know
What's here involved; what these kids did,
   Who caught more than a kiss
Though on some profounder plane
   There's nothing much to miss.
Six tall flights up, the pretty puss
   Leans at her windowpane,
Idly wondering which of us
   Will scale her stairs again.

RANK

Differences between rich and poor, king and queen,
Cat and dog, hot and cold, day and night, now and then,
Are less clearly distinct than all those between
Officers and us: enlisted men.

Not by brass may you guess nor their private latrine
Since distinctions obtain in any real well-run war;
It's when off duty, drunk, one acts nice or mean
In a sawdust-strewn bistro-type bar.

Ours was on a short street near the small market square;
Farmers dropped by for some beer or oftener to tease
The Gargantuan bartender Jean-Pierre
About his sweet wife, Marie-Louise.

GI's got the habit who liked French movies or books,
Tried to talk French or were happy to be left alone;
It was our kinda club; we played chess in nooks
With the farmers. We made it our own.

To this haven one night came an officer bold;
Crocked and ugly, he'd had it in five bars before.
A lurid luster glazed his eye which foretold
He'd better stay out of our shut door,

But did not. He barged in, slung his cap on the zinc:
"Dewbelle veesky," knowing well there was little but beer.
Jean-Pierre showed the list of what one could drink:
"What sorta jerk joint you running here?"

Jean-Pierre had wine but no whisky to sell.
Wine loves the soul. Hard liquor hots up bloody fun,
And it's our rule noncommissioned personnel
Must keep by them their piece called a gun.

As well we are taught, enlisted soldiers may never
Ever surrender this piece—Ml, carbine, or rifle—
With which no mere officer whomsoever
May freely or foolishly trifle.

A porcelain stove glowed in its niche, white and warm.
Jean-Pierre made jokes with us French-speaking boys.
Marie-Louise lay warm in bed far from harm;
Upstairs, snored through the ensuing noise.

This captain swilled beer with minimal grace. He began:
"Shit. What you-all are drinkin's not liquor. It's piss."
Two privates (first class) now consider some plan
To avoid what may result from this.

Captain Stearnes is an Old Army joe. Eighteen years
In the ranks, man and boy; bad luck, small promotion;
Without brains or cash, not the cream of careers.
Frustration makes plenty emotion.

"Now, Mac," Stearnes grins (Buster's name is not Mac; it is Jack),
"Toss me your gun an' I'll show you an old army trick;
At forty feet, with one hand, I'll crack that stove, smack."
"Let's not," drawls Jack back, scared of this prick.

"You young punk," Stearnes now storms, growing moody but mean,
"Do you dream I daren't pull my superior rank?"
His hand snatches Jack's light clean bright carbine.
What riddles the roof is no blank.

The rifle is loaded as combat zones ever require.
His arm kicks back without hurt to a porcelain stove.
Steel drilling plaster and plank, thin paths of fire
Plug Marie-Louise sleeping above.

Formal enquiry subsequent to this shootin'
Had truth and justice separately demanded.
Was Stearnes found guilty? You are darned tootin':
Fined, demoted. More: reprimanded.

The charge was not murder, mayhem, mischief malicious,
Yet something worse, and this they brought out time and again:
Clearly criminal and caddishly vicious
Was his: Drinking With Enlisted Men.

I'm serious. It's what the Judge Advocate said:
Strict maintenance of rank or our system is sunk.
Stearnes saluted. Jean-Pierre wept his dead.
Jack and I got see-double drunk.

GUTS

In its seat 'twixt bowel and bladder
Sits the nerve that insists he must dance.
Now he's tense, but what surly disaster
Might mar him a clean pair of pants?
No sense in anticipation;
When it comes, the man says, it sure comes.
This world holds small harvest of heroes
In its gross annual crop of sly crumbs.
Louse he is, but sustains the slim notion
Salvaging him even from fear,
Like curiosity, subtle emotion,
More selfless than first might appear.

When he was a big boy in britches
He got a girl in his daddy's sedan.
It was also the first time for her and
Almost over before it began.
Before he undid she was bloody;
What happened before he was in?
She was only paying her monthly
Wages to original sin.

He should have stopped there but he did not.
Was it courage compelled him to crime?
He was new, hot, hard; and he wanted
To savor the treasure of time.
Bathed in lamb's blood, dried on lamb's wool,
Baptized Buster becomes him a man.
The spunk to buck distaste or habit
Learns you more than a good high-school can.

In a farmer's field five miles from Nancy,
On a dark winter morn, '44.
I drove back alone from Thionville
To Third Army Headquarters Corps.
This here field ploughed with raw furrows
In swipes of wide violent earth:
Two medium tanks held disputation
On the essence of death and rebirth.
On its slung treads one tank was flipped over,
The other a crushed can of beer—
Two beetles squashed on their cat-tracks,
Me the one live thing anywhere near.

I parked my vehicle by the roadside,
Pursued tank tracks o'er the spoiled snow;
Implored my morale to quit stalling
Till I'd probed the fierce fate of a foe.

It was rather richer in bloodshed
Than the lass in my daddy's sedan.
You can feature what can't help but happen
When fire grills a thin-armored can,
Such container containing live persons
Who'd climbed in as enlisted men.
If you think this pageant smelled holy
Then you can say that again.

One question, one answer, acquits us;
Caught cheating, we only confess:
"Who the hell do you think you are, man?"
"No worse than that bloody mess."
They're dead and I'm living: it's nonsense.
They're shattered; I'm whole: it's a lie.
Between us, identification:
I am you, men; and, men, you are I.
Tests of failure, dishonor can hardly
Be matters of all-out degree.
Fresh earth will smother you sweetly;
A warm bath can take care of me.
Gruesome glimpses we stare down, maintain us,
Sin and squalor partly appeased.
Such scale bravery may even sustain us,
Our psyches released or increased.

We've endured the Worst That Can Happen.
Hallelujah! There can't be much more,
But the ghastly surprises of history
Hide their inexhaustible store,
And exams in a peace that we pray for
Make dunces of scholars at war.

VAUDEVILLE

Pete Petersen, before this bit, a professional entertainer;
He and a partner tossed two girls on the Two-a-Day,
Swung them by their heels and snatched them in mid-air,
Billed as "Pete's Meteors: Acrobatic Adagio & Classical Ballet."

His vulnerable grin, efficiency, or bland physique
Lands him in Graves' Registration, a slot few strive to seek.
He follows death around picking up pieces,
Recovering men and portions of men so that by dawn
Only the landscape bares its wounds, the dead are gone.

Near Echternach, after the last stand they had the heart to make
With much personal slaughter by small arms at close range,
I drive for an officer sent down to look things over.
There is Pete slouched on a stump, catching his wind.

On your feet: salute. "Yes, sir?"
"Bad here, what?" "Yes, sir."

Good manners or knowing no word can ever condone
What happened, what he had to do, has done,
Spares further grief. Pete sits down.
A shimmering pulsation of exhaustion fixes him
In its throbbing aura like footlights when the curtain rises.

His act is over. Nothing now till the next show.

He takes his break while stagehands move the scenery,
And the performing dogs are led up from below.

TRIP TICKET

Implacable fireworks bang wide-eyed in bursting;
    Fat young clouds of shocked smoke and red-orange fire
Hoist fingers from steering and freeze them. The first thing
    To blow is my right rear tire.

Mortars square in; I'm sighted in their magnetic vector.
    Small comfort to know in all fairness I really am not—
Their trajectory sprays any object moving in this sector
    For a random rhetorical shot.

Boy: you'd better jump. Jeeps are cheaper than you are.
    Slow motion drags its loose lurch, taut tympani pounding;
This man's torso subtracting thrusts forward, bounds too far
    To cushion the jounce in grounding.

My four-wheeled bargain takes off from its dizzy roadbed,
    Skips a pert miniature loop-the-loop in mid-air,
Flops gently to settle in orchard, its load dead
    On all fours, somersaulting where

Percussion subsides, though silence is patent deception.
    Tense, but intact, risk a cursory look all around:
No bad breaks—safety windshield the solo exception,
    Smashed when its frame hit the ground.

Next problem: how to get back without actually paying
    A worse price than shifting my one stubborn spare?
Two bursts tersely boast they haven't quit playing.
    Clamber under my car; lie there

Confused by so outlandish a manifestation:
    Who'll ever believe I turned turtle landing all but upright?
A shattered windshield offers no plausible documentation.
    When I drag in, way past midnight

Motorpool sergeant is snoring till morning inspection.
    I must fill out a trip ticket with some wild story or other,
Less lurid than truth, which prompts the sobering reflection:
    The inexplicable is a bother.

DP'S

In boxcars displaced persons howl hymns of home like wolves at bay.
Accordions support their choir: *Praschai*. We're cast on song, away.
For them it seems all holiday. For those in charge, quite something less—
Insuring thirteen hundred souls plus their accumulating mess
Leave a point north of nearly here, a treasure hunt which ends in hell,
For an undetermined turn on a blind gear-stripped carousel,
To hit a siding where ten trucks with bread and blankets lie in wait.
Estimate movement: twenty-eight hours. We are forty-eight hours late.

Paragraph 1, Subsection 1: the hypodermic numbing cold,
Far worse for them in open cars, infant or pregnant, sick or old.
Subsection 2: electric fright. Each scheduled stop an ambush seems
To petrify their timid guard and verify my livid dreams.
Boy with a granulating wound has dropped his pants for Doc to see—
My flashlight white upon his red; my hand that holds it shaking me.
The halts. The starts. The startling stops. Their wailing tunes and tundra wails;
Then, to surpass apocalypse, at 2:13 the train derails.

Its shuddered brakes. Disaster sure. It cannot be as bad as this,
While all it means to our dazed mob is one more chance to grab a piss.
The shy sun, blinded, oversleeps. Dawn, like our train, 's derailed by night.
A wrecking crew arrives by five to bang in a blaze of target light.
I do not care who else is slain; from strafing spare the undersigned:
"Where did you put my goddamned gun?" "I'm sorry, sir. I've lost my mind."
For cheap insurance let us bet where lucky Jerry's falcon-burst
Can easiest ignite our gas to repay worry with the worst.

The worst is spared us. Nigh on noon, the switch is patched, engines put-put.
We're really rolling. Feel them wheels. Sit still, my heart. Unknot, my gut.
Thus, o'er eroded Europe's map, her bridges blown, her signals crossed,
Filter ten thousand scrambled trains, unclocked and aimless; shunted, lost.
All you who catch the 8:18 to make your office sharp by nine
Consider your timetable may rarely correspond to mine,
Where Mars the testy anarch tortures unscheduled stateless cars
To give thumbscrews the one twist more he keeps for first-class global wars.

JOSEPH JONES, JR.

A **bit** bigger than most, this athletic specimen was quite complete
In pectoral, bicep, and deltoid, stoutly spanning six spruce feet;
Firm as a sound birch, it would take unseasonal storms to shake him;
Brisk as a diet of wheat-germ and ball-game could make him.

A big boy, big all over; big hands, big chest, very big heart;
Impossible to think of him alone, always the most agile part
Of job or joke; the nimblest, most limber, while his special magic
Lay in being what everyone else wanted to be. As for the tragic

Element, which in so muscular a mortal is usually lurking,
It was only his mind one might find slack or even shirking.
A self-starter, always set for the kickoff, such stalwart physique
Is fated to magnetize metal. Dependent on an instinctive mystique

Of muscle, you have to expect strain or snap sooner than late.
At the rate he raced through this war, he wouldn't have long to wait. **102**

Adorers dogged him. There were problems, of course, but few if any
Seemed uncomfortable, perplexing, nor were there ever too many.

Oh, sure: some mornings he'd like less that nice face in his glass,
But self-knowledge isn't stylish; left to themselves, doubts pass.
When he decided he'd had enough of our routine life and inane duty,
I wasn't alone in being robbed of his baked-fresh-daily beauty.

So, when the word came down he, among lesser men, was very dead,
We felt his aura effectively pushing up daisies, as he'd often said,
Scouting perils, sulking days away. The most common wildflowers
Bless any path, cross-stitched by perennial suns and domestic showers,

Not at all unusual save in fulfilling the trim limits of some homespun form:
Personal tragedy. In second-growth birch groves a hungry storm
Devours boughs, strips frail tree trunks raw with the heavier ones.
Thunder. Chain lightning rips birch bark; gash and sap. Gnawing guns

Digest twenty-two summers to artless echoes of modest grief
For this Joe and his genial hulk. His quick exit tried belief:
He'd been so alive and kicking. When I'd first seen him, we were sitting up late,
Six months back, drinking—charlatans, wanly trying to simulate

Intimacy, acting friendlier than we felt, that tired old makeshift
For friendship. Then his gymnastic entrance gave us its real lift
Into the luxury of loving—spry warmth, more cordial than gin;
Physical attraction lit up our gang electrically, welcoming him in.

We felt: new and unknown to us, Joe: you hit the right spot.
Dead and gone your merit heats us still, like liquor, a straight shot. **103**

TONY

A **midget-type** Mexican stud, tough as a range pony,
     Was our Tony:
Eyebrows lustrous as silk; the eyes—ebony, agate, or steel;
     No phony.
Queer as a three-dollar bill, hard as hell,
He could tap-dance, sing, do ballet, tell jokes pretty well.
    Universally popular, never hid a thing—
    Take me or leave me—yet did he bring,
To some tense situation, sterling joy.
Tony was quite a boy.

Plans for his program seemed fine, though one might guess what could grow
     To a drag show—
Uncomic gags, too damn many male prima donnas and stars
     Only go
To spoil great entertainment. From the start
There's our Special Services officer, that old fart
    Who bleats: "We cahn't be dirty; we don't think *that's* funny."
    What's humor about? Sex or money.
Jokes about money in a modern war
Aren't what the men ask for.

Our troupe includes a baritone-tenor M.C.; a clown
     Like Joe E. Brown;
"Carmen Verandah" (no Carmen Miranda): Tony Marón.
     Her gold gown
Once was a bedspread from some inn near Metz
Where she gets the idea for this show: "Fellas, let's

Dream up some kind ole-fashion burleycue smoker stag
      Party." So she tied a crimson rag
Round her curls, managed to look almost cute.
Playing the quean don't suit

Everyone. Tony Marón played it exactly O.K.,
         The only way
To ridicule the bull shit we heard, habitually talked.
         When he'd say:
"Goohood Niight; Guhoood Mawnin'"—put us in stitches;
Invent choruses like: "All you poor sonza bitchez—
        We got you Surrounded!" or "Each time we camp this way
        Boys wanna play but Girlz gotta stay
OFF LIMITS." It's not witty now, but then
Amused most of the men.

Particularly those up forward. So, that's where we go.
        Our minstrel show
Plays Pont-á-Mousson, a charming old town now hotly aglow.
        We don't know—
Can we work here at all? Unload, try to kid
A collection of half-dead, shot-at GI's amid
        Intermittent murder. Fanfare. Several crack wise.
        Half a laugh. Snare drum. Footlights arise
Simulated by shells traced bright and clear—
Thrilling, but too damn near.

Program formally opens as Fatso (tenor M.C.)
        Brays "Rose Marie,"
Shoots two lousy flat jokes. A fruity trombone introduces

                    La Tony,
Who grabs at her cue. Dialogue goes
Sorta like this: "Hey you gotta fulla bag there, Rose
        Marie sweetheart; what's" (rolling her eyes) "you got *in* it?"
        "Just like you, sista: it's fulla shit."
(Groans.) Now: the chorus. In tutus, six boys:
Indescribable noise.

Arm in arm they prance in; ruffles flounce, pink pony-ballet
        Trying to stay
In step. They almost give up. Christ, whatsa *use?* But, justa same—
        It's a play—
Professional as far as place allows,
Though now time and place worsen. Through the roof of the house
        More spectacular spectacles Begin Their Beguine:
        Krauts, closer than one hoped for, I mean.
We better get the Christ outta here, man.
Whilst the Christ we still can.

In shellings, we're not allowed to crawl under our truck,
        But, what the fuck,
Where else is there to crawl? Our full cast makes its rapid exit
        With some luck;
Rip back to base, where we learn we're all crossed
Off the chow list. Past midnight, cooks abed. So we lost
        Our supper to hit the sack hungry, thirsty, and mad—
        Grease paint still on. However, we had
Brought laughs to an audience of grown men
Who mayn't laugh much again.   **106**

After such terrific performances, brilliant success,
>Artists, I guess
Might find the Real Thing can pall. Tony Marón, a true trouper,
>Nonetheless
The Dance still adores. Right after the war,
Runs to pick up His Career where he'd parked it before;
>Trots to his Union; explains he's been four years away;
>They say there's FOUR YEARS back-dues to pay—
And he risked his Life for his Land! SHE RESIGNS.
"Sign here, girl." Tony signs.

SNATCH

Stained-glass panels shed their red as in a chapel to endow
With rose reflection brass and bench, and bathe the bar in ruddy glow.
Exhausted though still unrelieved, some GI's lounge against the glass
To sip warm beer and drag dead butts and wait their rationed piece of ass.

Near two full hours before high noon but in this whore-home's smoky air
A stupefied narcotic pulse vibrates the muzzy atmosphere.
Too bright and early to make love; nervous fatigue harasses haste.
We've just been dumped upon this town. We've fucking little time to waste,

And vice versa. Here she comes, with nothing on but rhinestone drawers,
To toss her tit and wink her twat and cense her scent of musky pores.
Our soldier feels his courage stir, although he'd almost just as soon
Hang around, bull-shit, drink and piss, and make it back to chow by noon. **107**

Yet sullen dreams of luxury unspent for starveling months to come
Inspire a blackmail base for lust to activate our beat-up chum.
Though he's no expert, still he can manage five-minute stiff routine
As skillfully as grease a jeep or service other mild machine.

Slips off his brakes; gives her the gas; dog tag and rosary entwine;
Moistures distilled from tenderness lubricates the kinky spine.
Well: up and at 'em. Now downstairs, the other joes have had theirs too;
They're waiting on him. Buzzy and smug, beer makes 'em feel a shade less blue.

He slicks his cowlick in the glass; unchanged his mug her mirror shows.
His pecker limp, he pats her ass and blindly back to business goes.

BIG DEAL

Speaking of genuine characters, Major McGeek was a case.
One's detailed to every division. At our Taxeville base,
Tall, dark, handsome, we believed he shat by the book—
A model of army-manual deportment and a common crook.
Marvin McGeek: to you I raise half a nostalgic glass;
I was mad to see Paris. You got me my pass.

You were motorpool major; a hound's tooth stained but clean;
I had to explain to an FFI liaison officer what you'd been
In civil life. Translating word for word, could one tell
Which was autobiography, which the bargain you had to sell?

Frenchy was begging that spare part he knew you kept in stock;
Your concept of lend-lease came as a nasty shock.

McGeek specialized in motor equipment. In automotive war
One thing most officers can't do without is a command car.
One thing command cars can't do without is a complex dingus
Of which he held local monopoly, which must bring us
To incidents attending Xmas holidays, 1944–45.
I didn't get to make Paris but stayed alive.

McGeek had been a big P.R. man for Better Business Machines;
His family is long used to service in the U.S. Marines.
Due to errors in Personnel it's still disloyal to reveal
He's sent to a mere service company. (Here one can feel
The charm, assurance, and enterprise of a talented thief;
Officers breed respect, salesmen valid belief).

FFI's Gaston withdrew, unserviced, with a Gallic sneer,
Leaving McGeek empty-handed, me gaping awkwardly near.
He snorts: "What's aching that slob? You do what you do;
These bastards rather lose their lousy war in spite of you.
Son, you're a smart lad. How about taking a flyer for fun?
I can spot guys with guts. I'm betting you are one."

Was he kidding? Marvin McGeek, wavy brunette, near six-foot-three,
Had not, as claimed, graduated from a good military academy
But indeed studied in schools of hard knocks and high kicks
Plus taking a few prizes in small percentages and the big fix.
I plead no moral or ethical advantage. It was clear
We'd caught the same nonfilterable virus: fear.

Headquarters' beehive routine secretes extralegal events.
I had guard duty. When the Lord God of Battles relents,
The awkward, craven, incompetent, or hysteric to pardon,
May he spot me in moth-eaten moonlight, drastically harden
A psychotic sentry's backbone, limp in fungal fright;
It was the classic locus for air raids by night.

McGeek stumbled past my post; I presented him arms O.K.,
He, a stickler for ceremony, each detail done the right way;
It was too dim to see me fumble in thick anticipatory gloom
While numerous indications promised imminent doom,
In zinc clouds, steely air, breathless X-ray stealth
Of buzz-saw noises inimical to human health.

"Hey, man," he gasps, "it's you." I smell his musk of relief,
He more jittery than me. It takes thieves to catch a thief.
"I'm that pissed," he moans, "I'm blind." A silly lie.
"You know where I live?" "No, but show me, sir," volunteer I.
"See me home, son." It's an order? Do I abandon my post?
Is this a test or a trap? All indeed may be lost

Yielding to magnetic attraction in this genus of male.
His intensity betrays indiscreet need. I feel him quail
So my valor rises. With less than a sketchy salute
I, carbine cocked, lead paths he shows. Then begin to shoot
Star shells, anti-aircraft fireworks, while grumbling thunder
Augments respect for ballistics in wide wonder.

I see him safe back to his billet. He offers gin to drink.
Noise has been briefly stunning. Its brevity makes me think

I shouldn't press luck too hard on this peculiar night.
Thank him kindly, tear back to my post, guess just right:
My relief man turns up on the dot; he'd been hunting me;
Palming it off, I joke about slipshod artillery.

Time passed fast. Christmas approached. Rain for days.
McGeek hunts me in chow-line, pulls me aside. He says:
"Soldier, you've drawn an important mission. Prepare
For detached duty for an indefinite period. Take care
Of instructions. Orders are being cut. You won't go alone.
But, kid: It's Your Ass; you're Operating on Your Own."

2

So, ho! for Paris, fair city of high style, cuisine, and fine art;
I love thee so much I can taste thee; my little ole hungry heart
Is set on Paree. In peacetime, thou art all things to all men;
In war, bright gold at the rainbow's end, wine, soft beds, orgies, and when
You're horny and starved any passport is cheap. McGeek said just be sure
To contact that motor mechanic in a garage near Point du Jour.

Paris! How many leagues to thy perfumed breast? Whereby lies my route?
We're in Lorraine, on her borders. Signal corpsmen only map out
Main highways. Metz isn't ours; the bridge at Pont-á-Mousson a worry;
But Major McGeek and me his man are in one hell of a hurry.
My Marvin trusts me implicitly, yet to tape it all supersafe
He ships along three overstuffed brass wild to get back to SHAEF.

Nancy is queen of our dark duchy, her artists sublime: Jean l'Amour
Forged floral gilt iron for Stanislas; Georges Dumesnil de la Tour

By candlelight limned Sebastien's corpse mourned by St. Irene;
Callot first etched the disasters of war, his needle tiny but keen—
Court painters to Alsace's twin sister whose sorrows never cease.
Eternal as art and suffering are, none warned me of terre-glisse.

Terre-glisse is slippery clay, mud laced in stiff oil greased by glue;
You float on its soup, you sink in its muck; you cannot navigate through
Black miles of sheer glassy roads with hard tires intended for tar
Surfaces. We managed at first and, leaving early, got even as far
As Bar-le-Duc, named for a delicious dessert, as well the former home
Of dukes of Bar and Lorraine. There, terre-glisse foundered in foam.

Our command car slid its fated skid; skimmed off the slick of the road
Doing drastic damages to our supernumerary SHAEF-bound load.
Driver was stunned; on the back seat, three officers took it hard—
Broken bones, crushed pelvis, internal injuries. My sole reward
Was, counting the hazards, a simple scratch, for, grazing the door, my head
Tore on its frame in my flop to the mud. By taillights, ropy red

Leaked through my thumbs. I tried to see how clotted gore would freeze.
Hyperaware, yet feeling no pain, I reclined in rich terre-glisse;
Finally sat up, ministered as I might to those more broken than I.
Aeons later, ten degrees colder, trundled a weapons-carrier by.
Emboldened by soft exhortations from Negroes manning this truck,
In no time at all we're safe and sound, Base Hospital, Bar-le-Duc.

When we'd quit Nancy for Paris, blithesome, insouciant, and bright,
Ninety miles north our troops and tanks bled in an extreme plight,
Malignly attacked by Nazis masquerading in GI combat dress;
The Battle of the Bulge's initial phase was a rabid loused-up mess.

For anxious hours, touch and go. Tall youth on both sides was killed.
Wounded, as many as might be sent south, Bar-le-Duc's hospital filled,

So when we checked in at 4:30 a.m., the place seemed black and shut;
Though bloody and weak, all I claimed for my pains was a superficial cut.
The pooped staff, at surgery since dawn, had just tottered to bed.
An orderly, looking up from his desk, cast a hasty glance at my head:
Did I require a surgeon, or might he lend his capable hand?
As for me—sure, anything, though I never will understand

How capillaries cram a scalp; you can't credit the beakers of blood
Filtering through skin with no pain at all. My skull felt carved from wood.
He scrubbed it hard; the green soap stung. He looped a masculine stitch.
I felt hilarious yet grateful I'd not been left dead in a ditch.
He led me to the head-wound ward. There, all seemed drugged or dead;
Showed me the john; gave me a shot. I died in my boots on a bed.

In the morning it made like Christmas; tinsel, crépe-paper festoons.
On the ward walls thumbtacked cutouts from Disney's cute cartoons.
Some of the men propped up were shaved, giddy at tea and toast;
Screens 'round cots in the corners showed who were paying the most.
Hero lying next to me, swathed thick in his Pharaoh's trim cap,
Assumed I'd been at Bastogne too. This ironic, affable chap

Kidded about dem Poiple Hartz all of us were undoubtedly due—
"All of us" counting those present, which included imposters who
Had not bled with McAuliffe, who'd been bought by Marvin McGeek,
While the enterprise I got skinned in held its signal lack of chic
Which was later underscored at Chief Surgeon's morning round;
He created a scene by my bedside with stereophonic sound.

Surgeon, a Texan crew-cut with a temper to match his red hair,
Scanned me with a wrangler's eye; I cringed at his clinical stare.
"What in Hell is Wrong with You? Who sewed up your Lousy Head?"
He ripped off my loose slack bandages. I could only pretend I was dead.
Spasms of guilt adorned my gut. He glared at his staff; he said:
"How often you-all been tole not to use circumcision-thread

On head wounds? Who's the Mad Genius who thinks he's so damn smart?"
Both our temperatures soared to meet peak standards of surgical art.
"We'll fix you Up, and Fast," quoth he, my occiput throbbing to burn;
"You don't need a welt like a rope." That clear, now it's the next bed's turn.
Surgeon wasn't so hard on him; pats his Egyptian mummy's quaint hat.
I'm left to blush at the business I'm caught thus short-haired at.

Without a whimper of protest, fourteen stitches they deftly removed.
After-shock, when it shortly struck, this racketeer's conscience reproved.
Scar healed like an excellent reweave job; my scalp no blemish shows.
My records read it's an honest wound, good as got against true foes.
Scar tissue absorbs disappointment. For my shabby personal part
I never appeared in Paris nor got pinned to a Purple Heart.

BREAKDOWN

Upon a hillcrest in a swarm of snow
    This driver holds his citadel alone.
High in the cab, he's left to staff a truck
    And feel each toe and finger numb to stone.
His pump's leaked pressure; the battery's gone;
    This bus rolled up the slope but can't fly down.
He squints beyond his windshield's flake-sagged frame
    Where prism lights wink out upon some town—

Nivelange, Dudelange, Longwy, or Eich,
    Wiltz, Berg, Esch, Mersch? Where did he miss that fork?
Route 6? Route 9? Here's no alternate
    To the old drag from Pittsburgh through New York.
The shawls and veils of snow in whipping sleet
    Frost on the glass, reflect his cigarette.
Our next twelve weeks of winter wind and wet
    Lock his big wheels in their glazed slipknot net.

His buddy's gone to get him help. How long
    Depends on phoning for another truck;
Delays from blown-up trestles, scrambled wires,
    And the short circuits of unhurried luck.
He is a fortunate joe who in this dark
    Merely endures, nor strives to sift from night
Salvage in chill nor wastefullness from time,
    Nor worry comfort from his trivial plight.

Shivers and puffs. His smoke's hot dot
    Glows like a pilot light to feed its flame.
Time stops. A season sets. Night's blind stare shows
    Shut-eyed or open-eyed a snowy same.
Our chauffeur's dream embracing summer sun,
    Stateside hammock, and suburban green
Fades with his Chesterfield. Grey-hooded cold
    Mantles hilltop and swamped machine.

A KP

Tec 3 pulls KP three times in ten days: is he sore!
He'd plans for this night. They are shot.
No one loves him, less than dirt, and what the fuck for
Is this war? Death were better: a lot.

Then some creepy jerk, he knows the type well, blows in where
He strips grease from the pots of his silly platoon:
"Report to the captain in charge. Wipe your ass, comb your hair,
Get a shave, son. Snap to it and soon."

"So what's this? Goddam Captain, the Army, and God;
What have I done? They've nothing on me now nor can
I've goofed and not known it; still it's odd
My luck stinks since this saga began."

He comes off KP, gets shine, shampoo, and some sort of a shave,
Hunts his captain in a weak storm of fury and gloom;
Kept fretting five minutes, he worries himself almost brave.
Then he's called to a small inner room.

"My boy," his captain commences, "I have Bad News for you,
Be a Man; it happens to all of us some time or other"—
Hands over the sheet writ in square type and true:
DAD IS DYING COME HOME LOVE MOTHER.

With interest his captain surveys him. How will he react—
Quick breakup or stiff upper lip? So they stare yet avert
Orbs which mirror the soul. When a fact is a fact
It's not blink nor a sob; it's a blurt.

So: it's dying he is. I request, sir, compassionate leave.
Granted. Catch a plane from the airstrip at nine.
Twin snappy salutes. He shan't grieve
Till he's given a sign.

Grief lurks in its lair to unleash in appropriate season.
Adjustment takes time. As for Father—who he?
(This character, dead or still dying.) With reason
He asks himself: What's he to me?

He returns to his mess-hall. Lamps low, they're all nearly through.
His secret stays shut, though indeed some notice a change.
Yet no one dares risk: what the hell's eating you?
Clenched tight, he buffs a gas range.

Daddy, where have you been all my life? Now from where
Hidest thou thy hard face from thy prodigal son?
Before you take off for the wan thankless air,
Bid me know what I've done.

Guilt boils from his loins up the vascular spine of his youth,
Simmering liver and lights to their slim broth of shame.
Sincerely—I do not give one damn. It's the truth.
Am I wholly to blame?

I'm a heel, I'm abnormal, I'm happy the bastard is dead;
Now Mom, Bud, and I have a chance to live in some peace.
He surrenders to moderate sobs while his head
Drains with mucous, tears, and release.

This gets me nowhere. Blow my nose. Wipe my eyes.
I'm no kid. I'm a man. What is more: I am free.
Choirs, swelling the end of film epics, arise:
Dad, we thank thee.

G2

Intelligence is Common-Sense or Knowledge-of-the-Enemy,
     Hence due-in-part to birth-and-brain,
     A busted-back and growing-pain,
     Lorraine's long night and winter rain,
     Our rear-headquarter's nervous-strain—
Intelligence is where I pray they soon may transfer me.

My company-commander quips: "Fah-Pete's-sake-whazit-eatin-you?
     Ya stem from all them Ivy-Leagues;
     Ya doan-look-good in ole-fatigues;
     Ya'd make-a-hit in deep-intrigues;
     I shall-appeal-to-my-colleagues:
Fill out these forms sextuplicate. We'll see-what-we-can-do."

Miracles happen. Here I pine on secret-project off-the-track;
     It's how I help to Cross-the-Rhine,
     And I can sniff from every sign
     By what intelligence is mine
     Uncommon-sense is just-my-line,
Absorbing poop from two ex-cops whom we'll call Jack and Mack.

Mack is a bum from Alabam', the dumbest of all classic dicks.
     So-what? Police-work is-his-trade;
     His papers proved it, got-him-grade,
     A looey, too; he has-it-made;
     His biggest battle, whorehouse-raid,
Till he pursued such tactics here, risking stickier tricks.

A-ramblin'-wreck-from-Geogah-Tec, Jack's a rough-diamon' private-eye;
        He's bright-as-brass for sports at dawn;
        Surprised with brisk accusing brawn
        Faithless husband, the well-paid pawn
        Of faithful wife. Now has he gone
To more strategic enterprise with wider scope to spy.

Security-Is-Classified. Top-Secrecy we-gotta-keep.
        Mum-Is-the-Word they inculcate:
        Ya-doan-ask-questions. You await
        Ultimate-briefing soon-or-late.
        Meanwhile my work's to correlate
The price-of-liquor hereabouts—and, chum, it-ain't-so-cheap.

For dry-champagne (i.e., quite-dry) the cost in Chesterfields is—well,
        More cartons than you'd quite expect.
        Quetsch (plum brandy) many reject,
        That local liquor I elect:
        Six dozen packs. If you select
A blander blend, Bourbon-or-Scotch, it's any loot ya wanna sell.

Whadja want? We recommend our commissary repertoire:
        K-rations, tires, candy in stacks;
        Canned-ham, tinned-chicken, scrumptious snacks;
        Shirts, secondhand from-off-our-backs,
        And lethal tool and fierce knicknacks
Partial-security protects a tenderfoot conspirator.

I have-the-duty, more-or-less. I'm on-the-job. I fill-the-bill.
        I get promoted; duty pays
        In-a-variety-of-ways.

On one of my dizzier days
        Jack toddles up. He tautly says:
"Ya just made corporal, buddy-boy." Twin stripes; a dubious thrill.

Part leer, part mystic paradox reveal enigmas of police:
        "There's a black market somewhere near...."
        I am amazed, show it too clear.
        "We've spotted the black marketeer;
        He mayn't escape. This racketeer
Is kinda-coony, in-a-way, but: all-such-shit-must-cease."

Vow Jack and Mack, twain burlesque goons, a sister-act from vaudeville:
        "It's time for you to now know who
        Our villain is. Man, this-means-you
        (We gotta keep ourselves from view).
        The lad's a damn smart jig-a-boo;
Some frog-gang pays-the-fellow-off. Find how-he-makes-his-kill.

"So you can sock him easy-like, here's extry applesauce for bait.
        Peddle him bourbon twice-the-price;
        He'll hike it high and heist the ice.
        Doan-look-so-shocked. No-war-is-nice.
        This bugger wants a bigger slice
Both of gross-markup-plus-percent. Is-that-legitimate?"

The Economics I knew-cold; the Ethics were-a-different-case.
        Valor's a soldier's first virtue;
        Loyalty next, though to the few
        Obedience boils its bitter brew.
        When put-in-false-positions you
Reread-the-Articles-of-War and pull-a-double-face.   **121**

Our cobby jeep we heaped replete with barter-stuff of jungle-cheer;
      Jack slips me road maps and a gun;
      Mack swears I'll have-a-lotta-fun.
      They learn me rules, and No. 1
      Is to ensure this simpleton
Woan-nevah-squeal-whar-he-come-from. He swears it, nevah-feah.

The road to Thionville I took. About halfway it turns hard right.
      Terre-glisse is hub-high; weather, fair.
      I take-my-time in getting there.
      Just-after-noon I pull up where,
      Framed in slim birch: my brigrand's lair,
A Louis-Treize pink-brick château, some Grade-B-mystery's site.

I park-the-jeep and ring-the-bell. I case-the-joint. The-place-is-dead.
      I check-my-map; my-route-is-clear,
      No human-error coming here,
      Yet something's sorta-kinda-queer.
      I munch-my-lunch and drink-my-beer.
Anticlimax muddled in malt confuzzed a foozy head.

When-I-come-to, it's-almost-dark. Lights may not lamp a homeward road.
      I've gone-and-done-it-that's-for-sure;
      My-first-big-chance: performance-poor.
      Night falls, with it, the temperature,
      When an enormous Black-a-moor,
Electric-torch and Tommy-gun, straight from those birch trees strode.

"White boy, whadja wantin heah?" His manner, eke his voice, are low.
      I rub-my-eyes. So, here's-my-man.
      I hasten to propose-my-plan.

His mask presents a pained dead-pan;
    Big hard-boiled eyeballs now began
Dilation grand. My parley done: "Perhaps-I-better—go—"

"Ya-stay-right-heah"—this Nigra grins—"gimme ya gun: y'all need it not.
    Just-step-inside. We'll-have-a-talk;
    Unload ya jeep whal Ah'll unlock
    Mah shatow. Whadja gotta hock?"
    His eloquence commenced to mock
Worry in powder trains which wriggle up to getting shot.

He helps me haul my boxes in. He is an-elemental-type;
    We heap square cartons pile-on-pile,
    In annotating each the while
    His eggplant watermelon smile
    Bares tiger-teeth: "Naow, honey chile,
I gotta-Big-Surprise-foh-you." Mah spine is chill though ripe.

"So you hail from Intilligins, an Institooshin excilin;
    It's tough apprenticeship is Hell
    But stick-it-out. Y'all do-right-well
    Since y'all got-goot-goots-ta-sell.
    But, son, ya gotta rottin smell,
An foh a man ta stink like that, it ain't intilligin.

"Betya-who-sentya: Jack and Mack. Them two dumb-clucks ain't smaht-as-you.
    They doan know info that Ah know
    So lissun-to-what's-foh, although
    It's super-flew-us to say so;
    Podnah, to you mah-hand-Ah'll-show:
Unknown to them, unknown to all, Ah'm in ya G2 too.

"Under Suvreyans foh six weeks, Ah reconnoitreh you-all-three
    An evreh move-that-you-three-make
    Ah'd oversee an overtake.
    If you half-hep ya-getta-break;
    Ya eat-ya-cake, ya keep-ya-cake:
This-is-a-Proposhin, bud. Naow, ya-come-wuk-fa-me."

Ah sweat foh Sahjin Bookeh Jones, a whiteh soul Ah'll nevah see.
    No extry motion makes him blench.
    He treats-me-fine. Ah am his hench-
    Man. Foh him Ah win wine-and-wench.
    Ah speak some though he speak no French.
Intelliginsch is Common-Sench-and-Knowlensch-of-the-Enemensch....

W FFI

We found his canvas stacked in dust—weak study, landscape, nude, and flower;
One portrait whose well-studied mouth even gives promise of some power.
No date on any sketch is signed much later than five years ago
When the invader came to mar plans for his first big one-man show.

Then he retreated to a site whose cave and cliff he knew by heart
And organized a team of toughs to practice them in abstract art.
He hammered splitting of steel rails, modeled the clipping of high wire;
Designed for roads, impediments; illuminated sudden fire. **124**

In his spare time in hideaways, 'twixt tricks on guard or days alone,
Furtively he first detailed where beauty's sunrise vista shone,
But this was hopeless; always near, the hidden threat, the certain call,
So he renounced his art until he could devote his meager all.

Let us admit, who with disdain, not undeserved, regard this art:
Slavery to a hard career beyond aesthetics tore apart
Promise, pleasure, and that gift about which he was undeceived;
He knew art markets call for more than the notations he achieved.

But compositions in the frame of ambuscade and dynamite
Assumed the scale of masterworks hung on the middle of the night.
As soon betrayed as briefly shot, his pals persevered as he'd planned
Till alien allies, better armed, usurped the posts he first had manned.

Now, all that's left of him is here: sketchbook scribble, flick of taste,
Needless unwanted immortelles dry in a cemetery's waste.
St. Ingres, St. Corot, St. Cezanne, whose shrines our galleries adorn,
On stronger students shed the glow which in his eyes was barely born.

LOAD

Our dirty dreams in ragged sleep:
    Kick off that blanket, creak that cot,
And all our billet, ankle-deep
    In dry-lipped dozing, waits the shot.
Upon some secret siding trained
    Forty miles over the Moselle
Nestles a long-range railroad gun
    Which slings a two-ton super shell.
It splits some slumber, rips a roof,
    Priming our chest-pumps overtime;
Set to sweat out this noisy night
    We mark the hours' quartered chime.

I am a tube, dry at both vents,
    My molars ground, my sphincters tight,
But damp in oxter, palm, and crotch,
    A hose for cowardice or fright.
I am a stack of plastic tubes,
    Liquids and solids to transform;
Bundled in armies, my moist friends
    Frame our vast sieve to strain the storm.
One supple pipe from lip to prick,
    One coiled long loop from mouth to ass,
A modest million drippings drain
    Letting each pissy droplet pass.

These thin-spray every fluent fear,
    Greasing its shudder, gag, and shock.

Wow! Here it comes! Just feel this floor
   Rise to the blast, bend, crack, and rock.
Well aimed from forty miles away
   Are steel-turned tubes the Jerries use,
But the most harm their banging does
   Is stiffen us to self-abuse.
Waiting the next note from their gun,
   A hot hand strokes an aching hard.
Nervousness exceeding fun
   Jacks a poor peter to its yard.

All eyes and ears on fire, in dark;
   Livid the iced, unspoken noise,
Threatening to madden, stunt the growth
   Of me and my lot of naughty boys.
Kraut cannon crouches, skins it back.
   Self-murder's tool is terror's goad.
It crashes about three blocks off.
   Its big load splashes my small load.

LIGHTS OUT

In this cubed space, a schoolroom, our company settles for bed;
   Blankets draped over French windows where glass was before;
   Kids' desks stacked in the corners; we tuck in on the floor.
   A smudged blackboard still chalk-talks what makes four times four.   **127**

One low lamp throws footlight shadows of huge stooper and leaner
Shedding pants and shirt, unpeels the martial biped.
      Someone shouts: "Put out that light!"

It's been a hard day. Unlike most nights in this uncertain site,
    Everybody acts gloomy; no horsing around or noise;
    Reproachful fumbling and stumbling; some two dozen boys
    Subside towards sleep. No strength in loneliness annoys
The single soul striving to snooze alone, a state meaner
Than marriage. Self-love more than true love burrows right
      Into us fidgety men,

Landing us all back here in an old kindergarten again
    If not in wisdom. Won't we learn anything? I guess not,
    Except new and novel ways of getting ourselves shot,
    As if we'd no thought save to forget or get caught
In every trap we've been warned against, which we recognize
As sly boys schooled by enemy adults, trounced when
      We ignored their plainest threats,

As they did, before we were born, with no call to pay bad debts
    For which we were spanked and drafted. Deep torpid earfuls tell
    Who naps. Hard snore, grunt, snort, weak groan, breathy protests, spell
    Out degrees of probing the thick- or thin-skinned shell
Of dreamer or dreamless—chilled, untrusting; primed to be wise
But prone to stay stupid, casting pitiable nets
      Into the deep quicksand dark,

Trying to make medicine of suspicion or envy to mark
    A nightmare truce. So we survive, more quick than dead, but by   **128**

Dozing, not knowing. Rat squeak, cat call, lullaby
      Of ventriloquist blab or somnambulist cry
Learns how sleep leaks its mumbled lecture to transmit a key
To codes where gut or cough read friend or foe. A lark
         Promises, bright-billed but mum,

What we're told love sings like yet can't hum. Conveniently come,
      Lark. Sound off and save. But love is no wonder-drug which makes
      Dog-tired foolish ones sleepy, whatever it takes
      To cure the pain in the neck, the trots, or the shakes.
Damp and unbriefed, all of us wearily twist, wishing we
Common soldiers, eager for kicks, dazed if not dumb,
         Had the sense we ought to want.

Let's pretend we always will sleep wide-awake, all licensed to haunt
      Each paradise we can dream up. Everyone smiles. Soft bowers
      And built-in sofas soothe our all-out powers,
      Beefy, untried. Armies? Worlds—drenched in showers
Of warm intimate glee . . . yet—who do we think we are
Tickling such fancies, not meaning one word, then taunt
         Our failure to make it true?

I give up. It's not in the cards to think this through. As for you,
      Lark—trill that dawn, but let's sleep first. At least, let me sleep;
      Make these planks softer.   I'll start in counting docile sheep,
      Pray my Lord this bleary-eyed ill-kempt soul to keep,
In return for which, past billet or bullet, too damned far—
Stand to, supernal sentries. Unsought, unthanked, do
         What can be done for sleepers.

Germany

CHARLIE BOY

His family was exsanguinated, atomized, and aereated
In a predawn fire-raid on Berlin.
That he alone of nine survived partly explained his power:
He felt himself a destined morsel of flotsam and jetsam,
A choice brand snatched from the burning. So when he met some
Americans near Mainz, we forthwith proved him right and hauled him in
As jester, pet, and pest. In fair return, he'd indicate our
Grim imminent future. Long before he trapped us, exasperated

By status envies, a syndrome seldom dormant in his septic nation's
Permanent incipient madness,
I observed his odd anguish in a big kitchen overtaken
From an old Wehrmacht installation, handily provided
With castered copper cauldrons; two of these collided,
Spilling a lake of soup. He nearly swooned, absurdly shaken.
Mess Sergeant bade him sop the smoking stew, yet his starved sadness
Was such as one might spend for private woes, not on mere wasted rations.

Precocious and prepotent, floridly fleshed, downily upper-lipped,
Fifteen years, a fresh and foul-mouthed lunk,
Learned six four-letter words and like a broken record these rehearsed.
Mess Sergeant slyly pressed seignorial claims and taught him
Some useful lesson daily. Presently he brought him
Apt and eager as a silent partner to his comfy double bunk.
Sergeant in peacetime was a famous headwaiter; he disbursed
Ringside tables to crooners who grazed lordly ulcers and overtipped.

Karl was our baby's name: Karl Schmidt. Sergeant suckled him as his very own.
Karl didn't care; now was fine and clean
In T-shirt, parachute boots, stashed ten times daily. Man—could he stash!
If nights were naughty, cheap enough quittance, for they made him feel
He paid his way and gave him the full wherewithal to squeal.
It rid him of thanks. Bred for blackmail, not exactly mean,
He'd hold his peace for now. Later he'd take it out in cash.
We schooled his queer contralto to a singing commercial's mealy moan:

Parrot and puppet, ground out the hit tunes, his sponsor's top-ten winner;
We called him Charlie Boy. Vas you dere,
Charlie? Sing us a song, Charlie. Charlie, give us the ole one-two.
Charlie, a poor orphan, sweet and sincere as the songs he sang,
Lacking a family or friend, sorta liked to hang
Around our dayroom sampling affection; swipe his triple share
Of Cokes or candy, estimating by shrewd impromptu cue
Which idler's empty lap would let him squirm there, fidgeting until dinner.

It pleased our sergeant to promote his punk; tacked three stripes to his uniform.
The midget martinet infected
By poisoned patronage or *Führer Prinzip*, pulled spurious rank,
Commenced to give us orders. We demurred. Back he'd tattletale,
Report our vain rebellion on some shit-detail,
Stirred mutiny to murder. Sergeant, sensing his game suspected,
Sold the monster he had spawned yet held him dear who could not thank
His tutor loud enough for training him to sponge, toady, and inform.

He was corrupted. Between us all, we cooked his golden goose. Charlie was too
Much. *Auf Wiedersehen*, lover boy.
His sergeant had to break the news. We bet they wept. We knew it broke   **134**

Poor Charlie's heart, and all were glad to donate each his dollar
To ship him off to Christ knows where in a clean collar,
Another Displaced Person. When our improved atomic toy
Ticks twenty years from now, watch Charlie rally the German Folk
Slurping his next Führer's soup. Who gave him the first handout of that stew?

DAS SCHLOSS

Schloss Voss, built between 1600 and 1650:
Am I our first to arrive? Papery silence schemes
To repeat a stubborn after-image, pale and shifty.
Passing the gatehouse, didn't I see a furtive face
Where everything else spelled newly emptied space,
Blank, yet heavily pregnant? And, speaking of dreams,

Isn't this one I've had often before:
My host waits at his gate bidding me in to what
Funeral or fancy-dress held at the height of war?
This must be me, just on time; so is he, waitful
For whom? Me—with a welcome gracious or hateful?
Yet whether I've actually been here before or not

It's his mother, the Gräfin, who really expects me—
Ogress or angel, she's secreted upstairs, inside;
He conducts me through room after room while he protects me
(From what?) to a dainty meal fit for princelings at least:
Tarts, butter, cream, sugar, berries—a miniature feast.
In its alcove, the countess's vast bed. Does she hide

Under thick winter quilts from our warm end of May?
Embroideries, gilt furnishings from fortune and taste—
This great house an individual dynastic display
Of German legend; from story too, that witch in her bed,
Smothered in covers up to the chin, shamming dead,
Her boots sticking out black below, tightly laced.

For a moment I long to rip off her blankets but then
Doubt my mastery of chance in this fluid situation;
Dull thuds suggest she has several uniformed men
Upstairs or down who can make beds, murder, or cake.
I think it best to swallow her fairly perfunctory fake,
A feigned weakness corresponding to the capitulation

Of her sick nation, never, alas, too sick to die,
Freeing us for our fun. I accept a strawberry tart
Ignoring its venom if any; pass the plate. Her eye
Marks me nibble nervousness. Then pride, strength, shameless arises,
Fully dressed. Thus betrayed, her son freezes in crisis.
He's dismissed: strangers alone shall learn thoughts near the heart.

"You're a man of the world," she begins, and it's true.
"I can see you're no child—college-trained, gently bred..."
Shall I snarl: "Yes, ma'am. Grandson of a poor German Jew"?
But, being no boor, I urge her to get down to her deal,
Which is old as her castle, always and also for real:
It wouldn't be much that she wanted as so she soon said.

I'd agree. What she begged for was by no means excessive:
My house is historic. Spare my house. We would spare it.
My son is not well. He's wounded—this, overexpressive—

He is ill. Here she halts: a Nazi? By no means; *that*—never!
I'd been silent. I'd said no word. Were we stupid or clever?
She had little to fear. Go ahead: let her dare it.

Ask anything, everything. I felt hope rise like a rocket;
Can't she guess my patience is impotence masking as kindness?
I say: If she has treasure, let her list it and lock it;
Our arms undertake to succor the poor with the wealthy.
We provide what we can for the sick with the healthy.
My feeble fibs supported self-hypnotized blindness.

I wished I meant what I said, though irked at her wheedling;
She ran on, released by my bland passive behavior.
I hate to be needled, yet my manner encouraged her needling.
She asked the moon and, since she was as old as my mother,
And her son, that sad youth, was no worse than another,
I let them presume my vague rôle as effective savior.

Well, what the hell; no skin off my ass what becomes
Of this countess, her castle, this crumbling county.
But when American troops act more like bums than chums
They don't respect Art. I make my ambiguous adieu.
Thanks; just—thanks; if we ever can do anything for you....
She donates her last butter and berries as bounty.

I find my way out via echoing salon and hall.
Mirrors mock an insincere exit. Polished parquet
Scorns my shoes. In the ballroom, soundless footfall;
A harpsichord open, on which Bach's Goldberg Variations.
Something breaks in, pricks my spine with icy vibrations:
Only that heir of the countess, who begs me to play.

I can't, so he sits and makes music for twenty minutes.
Bach begs nothing but absolute all-mastering order;
Nor does great dancing, concerts of finches or linnets,
Fronds of fern, veins in marble, stars in their courses,
The core of design in excellent or malevolent forces
Which lords of chaos or coherence coax into a border.

I thank this young man. In some happier dispensation
He'd have been a close friend; nay, even a lover.
Impulse shoves me to the brink of intense declaration.
Music undoes me. I'll help him, forgive him, restore him,
Unite what is left of our lives, slave for and adore him—
But conscience or caution warns of possible bother.

Driving back to base, I rough out a report in my mind.
Suggestions aren't mine to make, although I may imply them.
Schloss Voss can serve as command post, rest area; we'll find
Ample use for bedroom and ballroom. I needn't mention
Personal problems nor bring to a superior's attention
The Gräfin's greed, her son's need, mine, nor how to supply them.

FESTSPIELHAUS

And haven't I also been here before—
In 1923? No, it was 1924,
The first Wagner Festival after the first World War.
My mother, of German descent, liberally educated me;
Loved Beethoven, Brahms, though not Bach, as a virtual necessity;
As for music-drama, Wagner came first, naturally.

When she traveled to any foreign town
She'd hire a carriage and we'd wander easily around
Important streets. Thus I memorized this same ground
Driving from the station, as yet unbombed, sitting back-to, facing her.
We'd reserved rooms in advance at that famous inn, the Schwarze Adler.
When we checked in they would not take us. We felt some rancor.

Bayreuth: Wagner's imperishable shrine,
Noah's Ark of song. Between each act, one full hour to dine:
Würst, Kartoffelsalat, beer; the trumpet's ducal sign
Bids us return to the vast auditorium, half hangar, half shack;
Outside, brick warehouse; inside, a wide fan-shaped barn. Rigid seats sweep back
Cramped steeply. Swamped by such music, comfort's no grievous lack

Where not only Deutschland but all lands swarm
To bask in the Rhine's shimmering gold, the Flying Dutchman's storm.
Meistersinger starts like a Sunday school, sounds calm and warm,
Less the gross Wagner, more Bach-like, and while Ma disliked Bach, thought him a bore,
Even she couldn't resist such strong antiphons, such solid decor—
St. Katherine's choir-screen pierced, through which organ-voices pour.

Finally—the sacramental end:
Full processions, solemn din craftily composed to send
An audience roaring to its feet, the crammed aisles rend
Cheering. Here emotional or political factors scream and shout.
Next to me, a middle-aged black-sacked Jesuit with a pug's blunt snout
Howls *Deutschland Über Alles*. Strained cords in his neck stick out.

Deutschland's metaphorical music-play
Performed once more, after defeat, on this red-letter day—
Germany resurgent, while spurning our naïve way
In fraternizing with late enemies, rekindles a chilling burst
Of song, prophesying, celebrating redemption by revenge: thirst
For blood: ours. German soul vows to German soil all the worst

Of what's happened since, bringing me again
To this identical opera house, now upon pain
Of death. One more war, a second, worse, world war. Thin rain
Drips through its fretted roof. Our taut tarpaulins don't do a lot of good;
My Special Services officer, née Metro-Goldwyn, thinks this shed should
Be a recreation area. It even could

Double as stage for our own USO:
And why not? Who won this war? Someone around here might know.
In 1924, quitting this hall was a slow
Process. As aftermath of that daemonic Teutonic battle hymn
All exits jam. An exhilarated public relishes its grim
Retard in leaving. My analytical senses swim

Trying to make art and evil relate—
Aesthetics ambushed by murder. Enthusiastic hate

Spills out its heady surplus, and so it grows quite late.
Ma is exhausted; hence we, having no hotel rooms, are sent off to
A small private home; towels fresh, the bathroom and toilet nice and new,
Reserved for Jewish tourists and kept by an old Hebrew.

And why not? We'll feel much more at home here.
So now I'm back in Wagner's house for a one-night stand where
They'll soon revive his Minnesinging, lending my share
Of salvage to the site's philosophy, invoking more the malice
Than the music: Beckmesser's stolen prize-song, rude envy, and all his
Apoplectic anger: *Deutschland Über Alles, Alles ...*

4TH ARMORED

Was I bushed, workin all day: thirteen enlisted men, one officer,
We tole to take this ole town,
Move in, set her on fire; place machine guns at the crossroad.

One ole guy come out; he says: "Sure am glad to see you-all."
I say: "Fuck you are. Git back in line."
Lotsa Heinies—soldiers, civilians—all line up.

I was so damn tired. This guy come up agin. He says
How happy he is to see us, talkin pretty good English.
He says it again.

I smash his jaw with my rifle butt. That kep him in line.

141

This same ole town; we know damn well womin was shootin;
Them kep soldiers in houses too.
Took this one bitch, her undressed, in unnerwear,
Some Kraut with her. We kill him. Doan know who done it—
Charlie?

Anyway—Charlie he slit the straps on her brazeer;
Two ripe knockers fall out. Was that somethin!
We want to tear her pants off, march her down the street,
But lieutenant come up. He woulden let us.
She'd of fucked too. That damn lieutenant!

Way into town we head up agin a plowed field,
A womin there, plowin. She didn stop never,
But a lot of Heinies start up across her furrows.

I'm a farmer. She was real good with that heavy team—
Two big ones drug her plow, Percherons, Belgium hosses.

We pot them Heinies like pigeons.
Two of em fall into her fresh clean furrow.
She never stops onct, jus plows two of em unner;
Guess she was too scare to stop that fuckin plow
Still I can't see why she couldn turn her furrow one side.
Oh, I guess she done the right thing.

Then one of them SS bastids. We didn take no prisoners after Bastone.
They come in on us there dress-up like real GI's. You hear?
This SS son of a bitch have his piss hot.
Officer, he say. He wantsa surrender to an officer.

Charlie took his bayonit (this Jerry didn have none),
An Charlie have him a Heinie bayonit.
Easy-like, jus let it slide
Past this mother-fucker's ear. It make no difference;
Still kep outa line; still wantsa officer.

Nex time, Charlie says: "Lissen, bub."
I say: "Lissen, man, you doan know Charlie."

Damn fool wantsa die or somethin; open up agin, starts it hot.
Charlie slips that knife in his windpipe like buttah.

Worse thing was cold. Cold, cold; all the time, cold.
I mind the cold most. Weeks we never git warm.
Bastone. We have two K-rations a day. That's all. No warmth.
Cold. Jeez-us. Particularly your fuckin feet.

That Colonel Abrams. He sure saved a lotta lives.
Abrams love his ole radio. He git him inta town;
What a lotta bullshit that man throw;
"Now hear this. Now hear this. We have you surrouned."
Surrouned? My ass, but that's Abrams.

"Hear this, you-all.
We have you poor sonsa bitches completely surrouned.
If you-all doan come out an surrener esatly ten minutes,
Our artillery, which have your town already pinpoint,
Will commence."

In esatly ten minute everyone come out. An surrener.
Like usually they do; sometime, not.

One time we lose four tanks in fifteen minute to some of them
Goddam Hitler youth with panzer fists.
They burn our tanks. Flame-throwers. Cooked. We didn have
A chance. Them Hitler-youth kids. Was they fierce!

We see one stand up with his girl, her about twelve, maybe thirteen,
Both of them with their type bazooka.
Charlie have his Heinie P.38. Wasn use to it then neither.
One hunerd yards, a long shot fera pistol. Hell, long fera carbeen.
Hot damn. That kid drop like a hammer hit him.
Later, went over fera look. Charlie plug him jus unner the left eye.

He was going to pot sister too. I guess it was his sister.
I say: "Charlie, doan do that."

Then this door. I open up, easy-like. Tavern sorta bar;
They sell beer an santwitches?
Inside?
I'm a son of a bitch if weren twenty-eight Heinie officers,
Two machine-gun tripods, mounted low, on tables—
Swing roun angle one huner eighty degree;
Twenty-eight men, all officers. I count three womin too.
I tell you, mac, I had a lotta things go through my head.

I riz my hand jus like to say:
"Not one peep outa you bastids. You-all jus come on out."
I do this cause I know damn well we have evrythin set up, outside.
Atually, this town was very well covered.

Them Krauts come out. They lef their weapons heap on a table.
This here P.38, the one Charlie got; he got it here.   **144**

Another time, a bluff like this mightn work.
Atually, these Krauts almos didn believe me or somethin.
Some silly son of a bitch start to open up.

We had 75's, 88's, 101's, evry fuckin gun you kin think of
In hills back of this town, listenin fer one shot.
They hear this one shot.
Christ: we start to fire, just at roof level:
One, two, three.
Then we hit a leetle lower, a leetle lower—an lower.
Special, we pick out any tall tower, like a church steeple.
One, two, three.
Man, was this cute! Like a typewriter:
One, two,
Three.

ARMISTICE

Rain runnels helmet, skips the neck,
    Drops, spits, and hisses in our fire;
We shudder in each leaky coat,
    Boots squelched to ankle-deep in mire;
Really relieved despite the damp,
    A dozen buddies here have come
To pool our mutual luck and thanks
    And sweat it out till we're shipped home.

Burn fire, rain rain; love, buddies, love
     Each other, sure. It keeps us warm;
Battles of braver joes than us
     Have kept us clean of scar or harm.
By good sports shared, the wet warmth steams:
     A summer's done; a war is won;
Our drizzle downpour's not so bad,
     And slight discomfort's not unfun.

Real rain is soothing, for it hums:
     Though weather's wet, still pluck is dry,
And not a fellow's near as mean
     As I deemed you or you deemed I.
Do not misprize our meager blaze
     Snapping the short slant summer night;
Tinder love may still catch fire
     To kindle on the next sunlight:

Keep if we can some tender trace
     To carry back to bed again
Salvage of twenty piss-poor months,
     Copper embers in the rain.

PEACE

This was the end of a war:
    Here we were, rounding the bend,
Racing towards peace against time,
    Wild to be in at the end.
The front swept ahead like a flood
    Rolling away from our road;
We chased after the fading guns
    With hope our heaviest load.

For years we'd been one and one—
    Millions of ones, all apart;
The end of this war which everyone won
    Was time to unbuckle the heart.

Only a small border town;
    Bright banners hung to the ground;
Weather sighed thanks, everyone laughed,
    Brooks made a bubbly sound.
They said: "Take any bed here.
    Bathe in the brook by the gate.
Sleep through the steep or fading star.
    Don't wake up till it's late."

I walked into a white room
    And found me a big double bed.
On its fresh crisp counterpane
    Glowed a curly gilt double head.

Its four lips made one mouth:
    His firm tawny arm lay free
Across the pulse of her childish breast.
    They were not startled by me.
I sat on the edge of their bed,
    Held his open hand in my hold;
Our fingers joined beneath the weight
    Of her fair hair's curly gold.

Linen sheets fold back from flesh;
    Tan skin is kissed by white.
Here's where we've all come to play
    Tonight and every night.

ARTS & MONUMENTS

We woke up early one morning. My! what a gorgeous day!
We'd crossed Germany's borders to capture a German May;
    Strawberries-in-wine was the weather. All outdoors smelled of fresh heather,
        And my puffy captain had a lousy toothache.

"Get me a dentist; it's an order. This pain's just got to stop."
As dentists, we know the Germans rank at the absolute top,
    But this town was banged all to hell. I didn't speak German too well,
        And where does a good dentist hide out anyway?

Believe it or not, Captain's toothache led to our pulling first prize:
In the street strayed a blond kid with bangs willing to fraternize.
    I puff out my cheeks and I make dumb show like I got a toothache;
        Flirting, I proffer him three sticks of Pep-O-Mint.

With glee he snatched *kaugummi*, the enemy infants' treat;
He grabbed my hand in both his paws. In step, we chewed down the street.
    O'er a door of Gothic design hung a tooth as gilt ensign.
        The dentist inside spoke quite good Rhenish Englisch.

Captain's wisdom tooth was impacted. Dentist was tops at his trade;
He gabbled more than a barber but his tedious small talk paid—
    Much of it rumor or hot air, but somehow he'd been everywhere
        In the vicinity and really knew plenty.

He was swift to uncover our personal specialized part
In these dubious battles. We protected objects of art
    And here the coincidence was extraordinary because
        His own soldier son was in the same business.

No longer a soldier, he'd resigned from the Wehrmacht as such.
His uniform hung in his garderobe; his Lüger he would not touch.
    From his intellectual looks and high shelves of standard art books,
        Big ones, with pictures, he seemed a bona-fide expert.

It took tea and twenty minutes to learn what he had been.
He sent his French wife and child from the room. She brought cognac in.
    So: our war had not taken place. I tried to decipher his face:
        Kind? Dangerous? Servile? Clever? Or quite hopeless? **149**

He'd done his whole duty in Paris, charged with Enemy Art—
Location, salvage, seizure, and sale, all from the very start.
    He'd records of everything done since the project had been begun
        To loot Europe in honor of Hitler's mother.

His price was safe-conduct for himself, his child, and winsome wife—
How should I know this requirement determined a family's life?—
    In return for which he would tell which Jews had been forced to sell
        What, for how much, and where it all was presently.

We couldn't insure his protection. Why had he need of the same?
Urgency clouded his liquor as if some shadow of blame
    Disturbed this anxious charming chap. He explained it as mere mishap:
        Five years he'd been an officer in the SS.

Him! An attractive Prusso-Balt, yet major of dread SS!
Sentiments evinced by confession we'd just better suppress.
    His Courvoisier made us warm. There seemed to be minuscule harm
        Sharing first-rate brandy with such an opponent.

He did not conceal his status, conceding he might be shot;
Not by us: by the Germans. Beloved the SS were not.
    He felt we would understand, whereupon extended his hand;
        Captain lit a cigarette; I nursed my snifter.

We disdained all bargaining. Safe-conducts weren't mentioned again.
He turned over his records with the data copied out plain:
    Title, size, and the exchange rate; metal and marble, their gross weight;
        Catalogues of paintings, manuscripts, ceramics.

I was impressed by this scholar who seemed familiar to me—
Bonn-trained, took graduate work at Harvard University
    Under wise old Kingsley Porter; loved Queensley, his wife. He thought her
        The cleverest mad woman he had ever met.

His thesis had been research on the Abbey of St. Denis;
Professor Porter taught him to parse the stones of Vieux Paris,
    Which all came handily in when he led Göring's museum-men
        In heisting everything they could clamp their claws on.

At first you might think it theft, but later it merely became
Conservation as acquisition, if there's some choice in the name.
    Victory turned much bad into good. In all conscience we almost could
        Forgive his foresight as selfish convenience.

Interrogation ended on a brisk businesslike tone;
I felt free to venture a couple of questions on my own
    Since I wanted to understand how the SS program was manned,
        This type of temperament operated.

"When did you first start to wonder would Germany never win?
When you did what you had to do, did it never seem like sin?"
    In all hypocritical jerks, the query certainly lurks:
        Under just what pressures would I have behaved likewise?

At our first Norman landings he knew they were doomed to lose.
His answers sounded candid; 'twas horrid about the Jews.
    Of these, some had been his best friends; some few met depressing ends;
        At his club he found himself served off Rothschild plate.   **151**

We thanked him as we thought apropos, then bade our brief good-bye.
He recalled his wife and child, both beautiful, frightened, and shy.
　　He even remembered some more photos he'd forgotten before;
　　　　I loaded our jeep while he checked maps with Captain.

Was that the last of our major? Until about the first of June.
We'd been ordered forward May ninth and had to leave much too soon
　　To get the safe-conducts required. Besides, we were much too tired
　　　　To think of anything but important problems.

We'd all but forgot this Nazi who'd helped as much as he could.
His romance ended more or less as one might have guessed it would.
　　Despair at our lax ingrate haste propelled a predictable waste:
　　　　He shot his wife, child, and himself in a panic.

However, and all thanks to him, we tracked straight to a mine,
Masses of art inside tons of salt, near the Austrian line—
　　An upper-class health resort for Tyrolean winter sport;
　　　　It was now held by a committee of miners.

Lines direct to Hitler's chancery were laid to Alt Auszee
Warning to blow it to Kingdom Come should he be brought to bay.
　　These miners were Austrian born, held Germans in consummate scorn,
　　　　And weren't blasting their own livelihoods foolishly.

Mad orders phoned from bunkers of flaming Volsung gods,
But workers in Salzkammergut were betting on different odds.
　　They snipped all the dynamite wires and lit tall victory fires
　　　　Hailing the next army here to liberate them.

We prised open crates at random: contents not to be believed—
Supreme constructs of hand and eye that Western man has achieved.
    Objects like these are sacrosanct, for which the SS may be thanked;
        Everything promised is here for the asking.

In cases swaddled in cotton, Van Eyck's Ghent altar piece:
The Lamb of God sung by All Saints, its glint our Golden Fleece.
    Count Czernin's veristic Vermeer scintillates expensively here—
        He painting Dame Fame's portrait; we, in his studio.

From Bruges in Belgium one huge box cradled a Mother and Child,
Michaelangelo's august notion of the massively mild
    Carved in petrified clotted cream, a gently frosted marble dream.
        The edge of the Virgin's robe was chipped in two places.

The worst of it was when we brought out the Van Eyck for close view,
Over his hair shirt St. John's green gown was crisply split in two.
    We studied it under our glass. Now, how could this have come to pass,
        And not for the first time? Weak old glue feeds strong young worms.

How often through the centuries has Ghent's altar piece been cracked?
Obverse of its tempera panels showed which had been rebacked.
    Survival is luck or care. Excellence is canonized where
        It takes a miracle to insure miracles.

Time nicks St. Mary's mantle hem. It rips John Baptist's dress.
Science restores these losses. Art History mops up the mess
    While treasures get shipped home again to hang on the same hooks as when
        They were stolen by Hitler or Napoleon. **153**

Presupposing virtuoso vision—scratched, fragmented, or hacked,
Art's intention in barely marred. The residual artifact
    Glimmers steady through years or blood, enduring rough treatment or good
        Or the suicidal carryings-on of humans.

How marble moulds itself into flesh, paint kindles gold in shafts
Makes me witness salvation first in comely handicrafts.
    It's been often observed before: objects we choose to adore
        Don't prevent war but survive it and us.

THREESOME

There was: Corporal Harold Q.-for-Quincy Henderson and
Private (First Class) Leroy J.-for-James Costain. Each may properly stand
For any ordinary average American soldier, but
There are many average ordinary American soldiers one cut
Above or below given norms. Averages need surveys to sell,
And your survey tells every sort of lie about our moderate hell.

Theirs was not hell at all, at the first. It was sheer pure heaven,
Though anyone with a trace of brain who can throw 7-come-11
Might have learned from shooting craps that snow-jobs can't last forever,
While payment is fiercely exacted in kind when, then, and wherever:

A railroad-crossing six kilometers from Hartsholz GHQ
Had a little white-washed peasant-type wooden guardhouse and two

Gables framed with shutters for one bedroom and a window box
Full of blossoms plus one well-stacked babe built-in to cook and wash their socks.

Convenient? My ass. What a setup! She made rabbit stew
Their first night, and wow: was she marvelous! It only goes to show you
After so much shit you've had it up to here—well, man, it's then
God and/or luck, fate, circumstance, coincidence, chance—what all you men
Implore in awful hours as solace or savior—busts right in!

Costain and Henderson never tasted such sweets. Assuredly, sin
Sniffed its bit about. Henderson was Presbyterian born,
And Costain, Roman Catholic, but still stayed the dark relentless morn
Ten hours off. This girl, Mar-ee-ya, not Mar-ee, made beds
Or, rather, one enormous one with fresh sheets for three hot sleepy heads.
It had been better had she a sister, but even this way
Was quite the maddest night any of them played such mature play;
She was good and Harold no slouch, while Leroy, generous man,
Watching those two at games admired Harold's pocket-Herculean can:
That's what basketball does for you; then took his turn, and slow, too.

Maria wasn't the virgin American crusaders deserve, that's true.
But she had all her marbles. While watching Henderson make out,
Costain mused: The prettiest sights on earth often you can't talk about.
He should have meant what he said; instead, told some intimate friends
What went on in that railway hut. Ah, vanity certainly tends
To delete from grace each of us. They were screwed chewed stewed tattooed
And never had it so good. Close friends whom they told never understood
That when rumor uncoils, in the long run, then close friends must pay.

While Costain and Henderson did full duty at their crossing by day,   **155**

Pleasuring by night, circumstances past control at GHQ
Were forming a mean premonitory thundercloud which at first view
Was smaller than a man's hand which is what Costain often put
Under Maria's bust or fraternally on his buddy's tight butt.

Sharing is relief, man to man. But come—enough of all that;
There are certain limits beyond which one must not trespass, which is what
Lieutenant George T.-for-Tomlinson Kinicutt swore when told
Something damn queer went on in that railroad hut. Our adult kids were sold
By vain boasting. No one pardons any one or thing in war,
And George Tomlinson was Lieutenant Kinicutt to give what-for
To each and all who hadn't learnt his lore of how you better spell hell. . . .

The rest of this fable is guessable, depressing; messy as well—
A sordid comedy. At once he had them up on charges
Including: Sleeping-on-Guard, Raping-the-Enemy which enlarges
On horror, for, consulting our Judge Advocate's clever boy
He tacked on Malfeasance-of-Funds, Suspicion-of-Sodomy. Destroy
Evil where manifest. He threw the book at those hapless two
Who were now low as once happy high. Hard doom plus deep disgrace ensue.

Before court-martial he had words with Maria, that same whore
Who might also be blamed, in twin interviews. First: absolutely swore
Nothing went on but mend their socks, make their bed, but soon enough
She allowed as how she loved them; they sincerely loved her. This made it rough.
She shot the works, for which Lieutenant was grateful. Her soft touch
Made him selflessly eager to set her up for himself, although much
Of what made him hound these three trivial tramps for their puerile game
Were thoughts of Costain and Henderson cooling off, and in the same

Bed, which was what Henderson and Costain recalled when all shame and blame
Were wiped out—after stockade, dishonorable discharge, their
Forfeiting all rights, privileges, GI Bill—hard burdens to bear.

They bore them, then. Now, sometimes, their kids worry some why their dad
Often gets vague talking about wars which seem less exciting than sad.

"DEAR JOHN

Dear John" such letters begin; thus ever they're styled to begin.
Her's starts "Dear Russell" since she knew her helpmate as Russ.
"I don't know how to say it; still it has to be said.
After you read this I guess you'll wish I was dead.
Russ, this is the end of us."

Russ takes it hard: on the chin;
Continues decoding her skimped script straight through;
Figures how long this took her to write, which draft it was:
"It hurts me as much or more than it must hurt you because,
Russell, believe it or not, I sincerely hate to hurt you.

"Please understand." He does; if he bites his lips harder, they'll bleed.
She writes further: "Larry's on the late swing shift with me.
He has his car. I have no car now. I need a car.
I don't blame you, but the factory's so darn far.
Larry acted real kindly."

Larry. . . . Russ quite feels her need;
Still and all, Geez-us, he'd not dreamt it of her.
In his gorge two syllables start to flutter: You Bitch!
Up to now his lips won't mutter aloud this last curse which,
If uttered in air, proclaims all is, actually, Over.

What's Regulation for rage? See Chaplain, get laid, drink some drinks—
In that order. With Russ our s.o.p. is reversed.
Cut grain-alcohol with canned prune-juice. It's not so bad,
Or anyhoo, here and now, that's all to be had
To drench so drastic a thirst:

Stones himself stinko, then thinks
Of nearby supplies of available ass
Which are handy indeed. He takes off, rents him a piece
Perfumed like them raw prune-juice slugs. Therapeutic release
Does not pleasure a partner when she feels how plastered he is.

Chaplain remains. Cur-iced! Feature our shorn lamb back in the fold;
He'll shit or go blind. Chaplain's an ole YMCA man;
Human as Hell, boasting a brain though minus a ball,
"Wid a veree small peckah an' no ballzatall,"
Yet shall do the best he can.

Firm handclasp, supersmile: "Old
Man, sit down. Light a Lucky. Take Your Time.
Nothing's Bad As It Seems. Let's try and work this one: Out."
Russell sips silence; hopes if he pops, he won't scream or shout.
Unfolding her creased page, he surrenders the map of a crime.   **158**

Chaplain's read such piteous epistles before. This here's no shock,
Which he shall not admit to his client now waiting.
Muted thoughts buzz like bees but distil little honey.
"Son, I can't blame you for not finding this funny;
Still, it's no cause for hating

"Your wife." Broth-urr. "Now, you talk
A bit about: yourself. How you feel right now....
How you *do* feel, not how you're supposed to be feeling."
Risky business: Chaplain, a gambler, is appealing
To Intelligence more than mere Manhood or Pride. Anyhow,

Something clicks. Indignation halts in its tracks. Motors begin
Modest motion. Chaplain's aware of this ignition:
"I'll bet you already got pissed and laid, otherwise
How come see *me?*" Wide extrude Russell's grey-green eyes
With sly roguish admission.

"I know a speck about Sin.
It's my job—even, some days, a trace boring.
We try to help, but what can we do? Just take your case:
What do I try to say? Solve the problem or save the face?
'Fess up. When she was faithful to you, you never went whoring?"

Russell's rocked back on his heels, whose heels are fairly well-rounded.
How does he knows all this? For once, the padre's inspected:
Smart lad; bet he played halfback for his seminary;
He don't smell like no usual sky-pilot fairy;
There's always— the Unexpected.   **159**

Thus Russ feels an unbounded
Admiration, almost sheer, like attraction;
Smiles: "Sir, you're So Right. So what do you think I should *do?*
Take her *back?*" Chaplain mildy sighs: "Son, she is through with you,"
Waits; puffing at peace; observes Russell's unraveling reaction.

Russ tries thought in depth. Self-pity precludes guilt for transgression.
"You're so right. I'm out." Misery fills its fat bucket.
"A Good Guy, like me—Bitch. Now I said it, I mean it."
Starts picturing Larry. "I'll kill her." How keen it
Cuts. Stop thinking. Oh—fuck it!

What's the Final Impression
Left on the Chaplain? Russ rises, as if to
Make like leaving, sure he'll be asked to sit down again;
Cap in hand, lingers, lost. He feels the world's hate; his own pain.
Somehow he's landed up in the wrong, which he hates. This is new

And novel—analysis—rarely his self-chosen weapon.
Will his wan grin kindle a kindlier confessor?
"Sir, thanks for your time," yet this thin curtain-line doesn't ring right.
Chaplain proffers a paw. In any prize fight,
Even amateur, lesser

In stature can still step on
Brawnier brutes. Concedes he's defeated;
Tries Exit-with-Dignity a trace too greasily.
We won't let Russ get away with all this so easily.
We can't let lover-boy lam out feeling one bit cheated.

"Son, you listen to me. Try using your head. Take a long walk
Through this pretty countryside. Stay by your lonely sad
Self. Ask this Self leading questions, of which some may hurt.
You're no angel; she's no whore." The man can be curt.
"Cut the crap; you're not so bad."

The End, that is, of such talk.
Russ commences his pastoral promenade
Following counsel, through Bavaria's landscape.
Groans with blessed relief. Was this one a narrow escape!
Reflects: In our whole interview he never once mentioned God.

Nor had he need to. Near Russell-Columbus new worlds appear—
Alpine scenery—low Alps beyond bud-bestrewn field;
Ripsaw profiles of pure peaks in ever-living snow.
How, here, do such big blue beautiful bluebells grow?
Begins to feel, nearly, healed.

And God said: "Son, have no fear;
Enough for today. Gaze around thee; relax.
Thou'rt well out of it. Behold my wondrous universe;
'Midst my multiple marvels may not the better be worse—
As well, the reverse? Praise me, nor recoil from anticlimax

"When it comes, which it will. Joy thyself. Have fun. Take a new wife,
One more wife. Yea, two, even three. Possibility
Entails children, love, hate, divorce, death—all; even these."
Sun swamps him. Dear Russell almost falls to his knees;
Adores Chaplain's Deity.

Our hero finds a new life
In this German field in the prime of tall youth.
Yonder shine mountains towards which he need now no longer
Wander. Long trek back to base, but he feels him far stronger.
A two-ton truck passing picks him up for his tempering of truth.

HYMN

Front and center: call roll of certain scholars who,
Not thanked too much, somehow saw us through
Mainly intact: splendor traditional—
Salvaging articles of bronze, silver, gold, crystal;
Men famous, others evading fame.
All merit mention in fine arts' name.
         Praise them.

First: our Supreme Commander, Ike Eisenhower,
Painter of sorts in pleasant times, our
Daddy-O in the unpleasing times,
Whose decent manner, common sense, justice, stump weak rhymes;
Who endured stupendous waiting,
Winning worst wars with the least hating.
         Praise him.

Patton's side-kick, attractive Colonel Charles Codman,
Champagne-loving proper Bostonian:

When we must champion some monument
This gentle man his gasoline and influence lent;
Good then to know where one could turn
Lest fragile painting fade, flake, or burn.
           Praise him.

Colonel Geoffrey Webb, learnèd British architect,
Ordered U.S. sectors to protect,
Drove to our Third Army territory.
A hard duty was then assigned inferior me:
Patton wants no damn Limeys here.
Webb forgives me when I make this clear.
           Praise him.

Hutch Huchthausen, Ninth Army's brave Arts Officer,
Slain in his jeep by a Kraut sniper
While driven by Pfc Sheldon Keck.
Helpless to revenge his boss, managing to save his neck
Deep in German lines, Keck survived;
Renowned damaged paintings since revived.
           Praise them.

Lieutenant John Skilton, no noisy brawny lad:
Sensitive; among loud soldiers, sad.
By ingenuity, guts, energy
Saved the best Breton primitive stone Calvary;
Without help, cool as a church mouse,
Salvaged, from damp, Würzburg's Treppenhaus.
           Praise him.

163

Kyoto's gravel shrines, Yamoto's cypress halls,
Clean glory still, unscorched by fireballs:
Langdon Warner strong logic extended;
Joint Chiefs of Staff further Kansai fire raids suspended.
Shogun, priest, peasant, tourist—we
Bless his bones walled in Horyu-ji.
      Praise him.

George Stout, Lieutenant, USNR, first World War,
Had been through this type rat race before;
Instructed me, Harvard, 1930,
How permanent blue is crushed from lapis lazuli;
Back in navy-blue uniform,
Well-cut armor for informal storm.
      Praise him.

Based at Toul, Lorraine, in a French border caserne,
Our colliding gave me quite a turn:
Navy? Here? Yes—with sailors not a few—
Busy bees in loose fatigues of deep navy blue.
Landlocked flotillas seem unreal,
Their hulls and Stout's skull cast from blue steel.
      Praise them.

Near Echternach, Luxembourg, we worked together
In harsh destructive winter weather.
Bridgeheads blown; hid mortars bing-bong-bang!
Bronze bells in their rocked belfry ring merrily rong-rang.
We note shot sculpture we admired;
God's unconcerned with what He inspired.
      Praise Him.

164

Man was concerned, however. At least George Stout was;
Cooly judged damage: bimb-boom-bomb-buzzzz;
Gravely proceeded to bridgehead 's brink,
Watched patron St. Christopher's head crack, tumble, and sink.
George Stout noted precisely where;
After war, hauled up, now it's right back there.
        Praise it.

One more river to cross, which was their bridge-blown Rhine,
Captured quicker than the Siegfried Line;
Navy no more needed, Stout shipped away
To Pacific theaters more useful rôles to play.
There, something happened to him:
Monument Officers' paradigm.
        Praise it.

When Bangok surrenders, the Japanese assign
Buddha's toenail to His Tokyo shrine.
After Tokyo's fall, Stout sees it return;
Saffron-robed Siamese monks reclaim their sacred urn
Whose outer cover is dull lead.
Inside five more lay this toenail's bed.
        Praise it.

Lead, iron, bronze, silver, gold, and perfect crystal,
One snug inside the other and all
Skillfully interlocked, cut fine to fit;
A masterpiece of packaging. The neat sight of it
Awed Allied commissioners here
Detailed as steward or overseer.
        Praise them.

With soft chaunting, fondling smooth rosaries of jade,
Buddha's bland prayers His mild monks prayed.
The white Western observers hung around
Tolerant of picturesque sight, peculiar sound:
Lead, iron, bronze, silver, gold, and
Flawless crystal passed slow, hand to hand.
   Praise them.

Lieutenant Stout observing this fastidious rite
Was granted a brief profound insight;
Doubting his level well-trained X-ray eyes—
Oriental magic stirs skeptic Western surprise—
Hence quizzed his five companions, who
Shared the vision he'd been vouchsafed too.
   Praise it.

"You saw what I saw?" Christians asked one another
Since smile or faint grin each had to smother:
In lead, iron, bronze, silver, gold, crystal
Reposed in rich sacrosanct vacuum, nothing at all.
Samurai blades had served as thief
Of no booty save Buddhist belief.
   Praise it.

Good *gaijin* manners sustain Gautama's prayer,
Homage to no relic very there
Just as six well-wrought boxes played their part
Maintaining dull mortal credence by immortal art.
No thing grand some thing was: nay, is.
Lord Buddha's toenail indeed is His.
   Praise it.

Scholar-gentlemen laud master-sculptor, -painter,
As guns sound off further or fainter;
Gold or silver brighter and brighter glow
Saved by gentle scholars from our fighters and their foe.
Melt, hot bronze. Iron cannon, rust;
Let no lead shot smash crystal to dust.
   Praise them. Praise them.

Viewers exult, idling peacetime through galleries;
Curators vanquished artilleries.
Praise those who prized objects above themselves.
Some won't arrange them tastefully soon on our rich shelves—
Nor killed, yet kept skill's live spirit
Intact in what grace we inherit.
   Praise them. Praise them.
   Praise them.

THE CHOSEN

Under scant shingles, this unwalled shanty, a brickwork's ratty shed;
 Wide open to airs and damps and drys—
 A vast mass of loose written material lies
  In heedless layers, adherent or scattered wide.
  It is our current tedious task to try to decide
 Of what it consists, making practical choice of what may be saved,
What boxed or burned; initially, what can clearly be read

Of all these old certificates, old records, letters, unfurled scrolls
    From synagogues of ten Dutch cities
    Weighing five hundred years and a thousand pities.
        Its presence, despite much ruination, persists.
        Its chance for conservation accusingly insists
    If only as common courtesy to the slain or enslaved,
Foundering echo of that planned obloquy which still tolls

Through Germany, where in more horrible sheds spoiled a richer treasure.
    Where do we start? Reluctant fingers
    Peck at the parchments. Mildewed, a limp scrap lingers
        Stuck to its rotten binding. Square Hebraic script
        Perfectly readable could I but read it, and tipped
    Between pages, columns of notes writ in late-Spencerian Dutch
As if some genealogist of lore and leisure

Collated these documents to resurrect places and persons
    Until war's envy stopped his good work.
    Sympathizing with his interest, I won't shirk
        Labor, however futile—assortment, salvage—
        Yet a fever infects me caught from such wide ravage,
    Impelling fury. I am perfectly willing to end all such
Untidiness. My touching these corrupted words worsens

Chance for survival. I'd hurry their slovenly, worrisome end
    Blotting out many meaningless facts—
    Bury them at once—scriptures, ledgers, texts, and tracts
        For tribal banishments or dietetic rules
        Of rigid scholars in strict proscribed Puritan schools
    Which bred a stubborn descent electing to trim its thinnest skin
Marking them, and me, self-chosen. Obstinate backs won't bend

Easily except to the unique judgment of One Awful Eye
    Winking at the success of mad foes
    Who choose not to know or read. My petulance grows,
        Flipping torn page on page, date after dead blurred date,
        Name on lost name, trying to relate what can't relate
    To anything useful, shriveled poor tendrils of abundant kin
Shrunk on the branch, rooted in fine granite dust from Sinai.

I con these screeds as if by fitful tapers whose curled fetid smoke
    Dimmed ignorance's unfestive light.
    They flare from wicks whose sick wax first makes flame bright
        But then ill vapors rise, swelling a sluggish pall,
        Snuffing out any legible handwriting at all;
    There's left a smothering canopy, an impenetrable haze
Through which no candles glow. Is it faith I cannot invoke,

The faith of my fathers—all those prophets, scholars, lawyers, ancients,
    Whose busheled ash sifts Israel's decline?
    Made firm our road? Why may we never take for sign
        The criminal thorn we chose to set as His crown?
        Let's prise it from His enemy head and lift Him down
    To lie at last among forgiving kindred. We pay; He still pays;
Maybe the solvency in brotherhood all but consents

Not to be chosen, while many Gentile gypsies and infant Jews
    Have no choice. Their ends are made less hard
    By their parents' playing games with their cruel guard,
        Pretending to laugh, who both shove them in hot gas
        And, waving, watch them choke and smoulder through the thick glass.
    They all knew it was never a real game. The guards were also young;
As for choosing, even the young gas-oven guards could choose   **169**

To push or not. Some let themselves be pushed and had no cause to kill.
    Old books bleach, faint scrivening left.
    Apart from calligraphy are we much bereft
        Of learning? Could I have read, would I? A choice text
        Compels little but quotation, awaiting the next
    Example of His choosing or chastisement, and psalms simply sung
Remember themselves without prompting scribe or saving skill

On our part, in cleansing fierce covenants of worm hole, mold, or wear.
    Ourselves chose; or were we chosen truly
    Improvising laws for our self-serving school? He,
        Unwilling to cozen His favored children, less
        From rage than to scourge us strong, reveals His wilderness
    Without a word. We praise, wailing; our temple, the collapsed abyss.
We swear, having borne much, it's more than we ever can bear;

Gratefully swear it; then bear it. Jealous vanity bids us hear
    Sacred pride in secret pride: Thy Word
    Echoed from desert utterings, Thy Promise heard
        Abrupt as thunder. Did we ourselves first say it?
        I am that I am. Fear thy God, thine: alone. Pray it
    Illumines the legible pages of wisdom left in all this
Waste. Call it mercy, these blank vellum margins scorched with fear.

Postscript

PURPLE HEART

Sure, he's lucky to be alive; those parts of him that feel at all
Throb in their frame. His eyes test ceiling and the blank wall.

His weak wrists on crisp sheets ache, though he knows he'll be all right;
Nurse gives him a sharp look, raises the window, dims the light,

Quits him. Darkness fuses; burns. Spots in his shut eyes spark;
Alone, he worries some more whether burns leave a bad mark.

He tells himself: The worst is over, doing what had to be done.
He did well, but he's not sure if the worst has even begun.

He tries not to dream nor yet doze on what all happened back there—
A bad accident roaring around found and froze him in its glare.

He'd been dreading it months—this menace, test, this end, this worst.
While he waited for it to hit, skies fainted and he burst.

Folks, at least for a while, will be in awe of him. They'll stand
Aside from him or steal luck, patting his back; wringing his hand.

He's sick, naturally; he can't ask what he needs and well knows
He hasn't the stuff to love back; fades into a thin doze.

Not enough love to go around, a blood bank to pull him through
Easily. He'll come out of it, the hard way. Myself, or you,

Seeing him thus are moved to tears. Real tears. We always need
Tours through the wards to make sure real wounds really bleed.

"HERE LIES

who am now but a thought
    Once was a fanciful man;
Blood in my nerve, skin on my bone;
    My cheek took a coppery tan.
While I was breathing I feared
    The nothing I soon might be;
Fun, like my fright, was fantasy,
    Sturdiest part of me.
Mirror grinned: 'Don't worry, Joe.
    Others may possibly die,
But boys with flax hair and green eyes,
    Fast workers like you and I,
Are so firm in fanciful pride
    The elegance crammed in our youth
Is helmet enough to keep us whole,'
    Which we knew was hardly the truth."

I'm thinking of three friends of mine,
    None of them selfless nor strong,
Who loved themselves far more than me,
    And fashion, excitement, and song,
Who now are deader than I,
    Who never fancifully lied:
"We lived for somebody else;
    For somebody else we died."
Fair Harry, red Caleb, dark Fred
    Were lavish in other ways,

And when it came time to be killed
    The flush of their holiday days
Spilled its fancy exuberant light
    On a shadow-long late afternoon;
Flared into dusk like song, and sang
    Ends to a fanciful tune.

GI BILL

So: here's our Joe back home again,
    And tart October nips his ears;
Nothing about his street or room
    Reminds him he's been gone three years.
Schedule the same: habit persists—
    Bed, bath, and breakfast; pipe and book.
Time shrinks it tight, a seamless stitch
    All scarless from the trip he took.

Ex-pilot wires his bombardier
    To hop out West and meet the folks—
A fortnight off for fish and games,
    Air Corps talk and GI jokes;
Whips back to college to cram up,
    Add or subtract what so far fails
To keep his classmates at their sums
    When fires freeze or scrap-iron hails.

Professor waits his heroes home
    Alert and tender to be told,
Astounded at what innocence
    Survives the stories they were sold.
For how can he, poor Ph.D.,
    An idiot AWOL from their war,
Venture to lecture veterans
    On what they've just been fighting for?

Each starved survivor aches to learn;
    Professor has no cause for fear;
Straining towards logic, every son
    Lends a rapt unaccusing ear.
Down the long wards, the walking wounds
    Compare their chances, legs, and eyes
Left to each user, all in luck
    Contrasting fiercer sacrifice.

Lo: the World Wars I, II, and III
    Now test our homework's memory;
Ten months ago what towns were tall
    Whose wrecks date Modern History?

MEMORIAL

By here, where once we came
Along this selfsame road
Back to our base and field,
Perennial pollens yield
Their ragged rusty fame.

Burdock, hard burr, and rose,
Sweet wildrose, dusty burr,
Thistle and aster wild—
Past here a waiting child
Ambushed some noisy boys

To ask: Where are you bound?
Where bound indeed? Where? Where?
They did not know, and we
Who know more than they knew
Have lost more than they found.

This chapel scarce a church
They could ignore. They did;
To them—odd heap of stones,
Old shelter for some bones
Or pigeons on a perch.

Thin and unshadowed shone
Pale panes of window glass.
But color? No; nor glint
Of richness, gleam, or tint;
No texture and no tone.

Why should they stop to pray?
They had their way to win.
They flew far, headlong fast,
Reckless and randy past
Broad daylight and brief day.

All gone. Some gone for good.
Some bad, some still alive,
While those alive, with grace
Have not forgot this place:
We've done the least we could.

We've stuck a window here:
Pure color for clear flesh,
A penetrating fire
To glorify the choir
Or sanctify our fear.

What are these colors fine
That strain the sun; shine clean
In citron, rosy ice,
Mulberry paradise,
Sharp wintergreen, or wine?

This fire is all our air
Which was our airman all.
Our window claims he's here
In warm translucent cheer
And gilt transparent hair.

Blond as the licking sun,
Rosy for tawny cheek,
Frank mirror-eye and green
His candid earth and keen
His fury in his fun.

Glass is sand, sun, and lead
Fixed in a shattered sheet.
All day our star is sight;
At sunset shuttered night
All dust, dust-shot and dead.

In four fierce sheaves of fire
An elemental shock
Has compassed every air
Boxed cardinal to square
Sky, ocean, flame, and mire.

Fuse us our triune saint
Who was boy, bomb, and blast.
Brittle his doubled arm.
Tense still our hard alarm
And strenuous complaint.

For glass, send us some sun.
Blend blood and bone a hymn
To salve our coupled nerve
Preserving us to serve
The wonder in a one.

The "weathermark" identifies this edition as having been designed & produced by John Weatherhill, Inc., Tokyo / Book design & typography by Meredith Weatherby / Composition & printing by Sobunsha, Ltd., Tokyo / Binding by Okamoto Bindery, Tokyo / The text type is 12-point Monotype Bodoni, with Ultra Bodoni and Onyx used for display